Loretta Santini - Cinzia Valigi

# PERUGIA
# ASSISI - GUBBIO
## ORVIETO - SPOLETO

Published and printed by

**plurigraf**

Narni - Terni
ITALIA

# Introduction

In this album we present five of the best known and most beautiful cities of Umbria. With their wonderful monuments, their fascinating history, their traditions, their culture and art, they are justly the boast of this Region and worthily represent all its other towns and villages – and they are numerous – which are enriched like Perugia, Assisi, Gubbio, Orvieto and Spoleto with exceptional historical monuments and marvellous scenic views.

The dominant note of all these Umbrian towns is their medieval atmosphere: the townscape that characterizes them consists almost exclusively of an inhabited nucleus clinging to the slopes of hills, with houses built of local stone and huddled together to form a maze of little streets and piazzas. These are often as steep as the hillsides on which they are laid out, and everywhere open up picturesque and unforgettable views. In all these towns a medieval fortress or the remains of ancient town walls, often of Etruscan or Italic origin, can be found.

In all of them, too, we can find magnificent Romanesque or Gothic churches or superb public buildings dating to the period of the medieval city-states – the communal places of the Chief Magistrates or Captains of the People. These are invariably sober and essential in style, but at the same time of the greatest elegance. Architecturally, they are based on features of Tuscan derivation, but strongly influenced by highly individual local tendencies.

Painting, too, flourished in Umbria in the Middle Ages and Renaissance: its greatest exponents were Giotto, who was responsible for the wonderful frescoes in the Basilica of Assisi, Cimabue, Pinturicchio, Perugino and Signorelli, just to cite some of the major names. The same can be said of sculpture, which has left a magnificent heritage in the cities of Umbria in the form of the decoration of fountains, churches and palaces.

The beauty of certain monuments such as the Cathedral of Orvieto and the Church of St. Francis or the Palazzo dei Consoli in Gubbio or the Palazzo dei Priori in Perugia, bear eloquent witness to the importance of these cities and of the whole Region.

To all this must be added the richness of their traditions, ranging from those concerning the local handicrafts which have a centuries-old history and have always been distinguished by their very high quality – especially those of ceramics and lace-making – to those concerning festivities and commemorative events. These latter, all of the greatest interest (it is enough to mention the famous "Corsa dei Ceri" in Gubbio, the various religious rites in Assisi, or the International Festival of the arts in Spoleto) are not contemporary re-evocations of historical cultures.

Last but not least, we should mention the enchanting landscapes in which these historic towns are set and which enhance them by their scenic environs: with its unforgettable views and magical natural endowment, the fruitful countryside of Umbria everywhere provides a worthy setting.

It is an oasis of peace and tranquillity, a landscape of gently rolling hills and olive-groves among which nestle so many picturesque little towns and villages, enriched with countless records of the past and all imbued with the same spellbound medieval atmosphere, the same religious silence, the same unaltered simplicity. Among all these Umbrian towns, Perugia, Assisi, Gubbio, Orvieto and Spoleto hold a conspicuous place due to their unforgettable treasures of history, art and culture.

*Above·*
*Perugia, Piazza IV Novembre,*
*Assisi, The Basilica of St. Francis*

*To the side:*
*Gubbio, The Consul's Palace,*
*Spoleto, The Cathedral,*
*Orvieto, The Cathedral*

# Perugia

Already on its first appearance, Perugia reveals itself as a magnificent and noble city with an image and appearance all of its own. Among the best-known and most significant of Italy's centres of art and undoubtedly one of the finest cities in Umbria, it lies spread out on the top of a hill, whose irregular terrain and sometimes precipitous gradients it follows, thus assuming a townscape characterized by the pronounced branching out of its various arms and by buildings which seem to be raised one above the other. All this confers on Perugia a highly personalized character, both proud and picturesque.

Yet what makes this city really wonderful is the sum of its monuments and works of art: ranging from the imposing Etruscan Arch to the marvellous Piazza IV Novembre, one of the finest piazzas in Italy, with its exceptional Palazzo dei Priori and Fontana Maggiore; from the many churches enriched with significant paintings to the complex of Museums of major importance such as the Archaeological Museum and the National Gallery of Umbria. Nor should we forget the evocative and truly unique Rocca Paolina or the series of ancient gateways that open up along the perimeter of the city's circuit of walls which date back in origin to Etruscan times. But above all what makes Perugia so memorable is the particular atmosphere, the picturesque charm, that imbues every street and every corner of the city: the narrow alleys, all ups and downs, that run in a maze through the centre, intersecting in ever-changing variety, the vaults, the arches flung over the streets and buttressing the houses, the silent little piazzas, and all that exhilarating opening up of ever different perspectives and corners of the town that seem to have remained immutable in time, colored by the dark patina that the centuries have left in their memory.

Perugia is a city that continues to live today – and with great liveliness – amid these splendid records of the past. It is a city of art and culture. This is attested not only by the many monuments we have summarily mentioned and by its history, but also by the presence of one of the oldest Universities in Italy, by the establishment of the University for Foreigners for the diffusion of Italian culture abroad, and by the various important musical and theatrical events that take place in the city.

Perugia's townscape is characterized by an ancient medieval nucleus contained within the circuit of walls of Etruscan and Roman origin which still runs intact round a large part of the city. Another circuit of walls arose in the 14th century to comprise the urban districts that had in the meantime developed along the slopes of the hill.

Perugia has been called a "tentacular" city due to the typical star-shaped branches of the built-up area which follow the diverging ridges of the hill. It is divided into five **rioni** or urban districts: Porta Sant'Angelo, Porta San Pietro, Porta Sole, Porta Santa Susanna and Porta Eburnea.

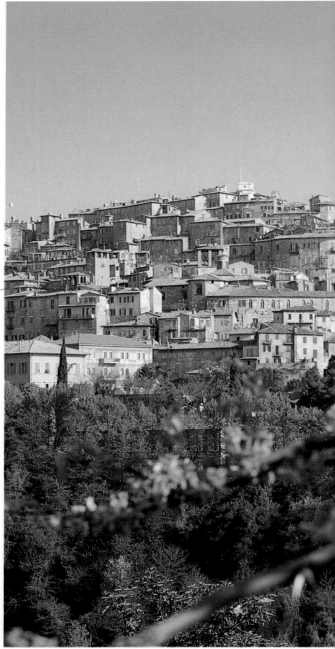

*Porta S. Angelo,*
*Porta S. Pietro,*
*Porta Eburnea*

# Historical Background

Perugia was probably in origin a settlement of the Umbri, an ancient Italic people, but rapidly rose to prominence as one of the most powerful and important of the Etruscan cities. The Etruscan ascendancy is eloquently attested by the significant traces of Etruscan civilization that still remain in the surrounding territory and in the city itself (Etruscan town-gate known as the Arch of Augustus, the Porta Marzia and the Hypogeum of the Volumnii), and by the variety and richness of the artefacts contained in the Archaeological Museum. The position of power and authority attained by the Etruscan city long ennabled it to remain independent of Rome; it only became subject to Roman rule after having been besieged and reduced by Octavian during his war against Anthony. The same Emperor, who had in part laid waste the city during this conflict, later promoted its revival: it was rebuilt and assumed, in his honour, the name of **Augusta Perusia**.

On the fall of the Roman Empire, it suffered, like the rest of the peninsula, from the successive barbarian invasions. Sacked by the Goth Totila after a siege of seven years in the 6th century, it revived and, from the 11th century, established itself as a free city-state: From that time the city began to assume the urban configuration that still distinguishes it today, and more especially began to enrich itself with magnificent public buildings and works of painting and sculpture of great value, attributable in large part to the 13th century.

These factors testify to the importance assumed by the city-state of Perugia in the Middle Ages, and are an index not only of its cultural prestige but of its political and economic position. The city in fact extended its sphere of influence over a large part of Umbrian territory and, in its expansion, frequently entered into conflict with neighbouring city-states.

While the 15th century represented for Perugia, from an artistic and pictorial point of view in particular, a period of great splendour (with the presence in the city of Raphael, Pinturicchio, Perugino, Bonfigli and Fiorenzo di Lorenzo), politically it signified a period of upheaval: the city was torn by the constant vicissitudes of civil strife and a succession of tyrannical regimes, from that of the Michelotti to Fortebraccio and the eventual ascendency of the Baglioni family.

The Baglioni kept their grip on the city longer than the other contenders, albeit amid continuing wars, maintaining their supremacy until 1531. This was the year in which Perugia, following the "saltwar" precipitated by a popular revolt against a new tax imposed by the Pope, finally fell under the domination of the Papal State. The Farnese Pope Paul III, whose victory this was, then erected a citadel in the city as a symbol of his power: the famous Rocca Paolina built by the architect Antonio di Sangallo the Younger over the ruins of the residence of the Baglioni family.

Papal power in Perugia endured virtually unchallenged till 1860, the year of its annexation to the emerging Kingdom of Italy.

Brief interruptions in papal rule were registered on the occasion of the Napoleonic invasion of Italy (1798), during the period of the Roman Republic (1848) and during the bloody revolt of 1858 which was savagely suppressed by the papal troops.

# The Piazza IV Novembre

The historic and artistic hub of Perugia, the Piazza IV Novembre is one of the loveliest civic squares in Italy thanks to the beauty of the monuments with which it is adorned, such as the wonderful Palazzo dei Priori, the Fontana Maggiore and the Cathedral.

# The Fontana Maggiore

This large civic fountain, the wonderful creation of Nicola and Giovanni Pisano and Fra Bevignate of Perugia, represents a masterpiece of 13th century art; the harmony and proportion of its architectural structure and the beauty of its sculptural decoration are fused together to form a magnificent ensemble.

The fountain consists of two superimposed polygonal basins, the upper one with a slightly smaller diameter. Below, the fountain rests on a circular stepped podium, while above it is topped at the centre by a column supporting a bronze vessel from which emerges Giovanni Pisano's bronze sculptural group representing **Three Nymphs**. The lower polygonal basin is decorated with 48 relief-panels, divided by twisted colonnettes: the bas-reliefs within them describe the months of the year, the signs of the Zodiac, the Liberal Arts and various biblical episodes. Yet the narrative sequence of the reliefs is not that originally conceived by the artist, since various alterations have been made to it over the centuries. Nicola Pisano, who is generally identified as the fountain's designer, probably intended to describe, in successive reliefs, an ideal history that, starting out from the creation of Adam and Eve and the commission of original sin, saw the development of the various forms of human work and, subsequently, the Liberal Arts; from all this emerged the birth of Perugia itself, symbolized by the figures of the Lion and the Griffin and also by the twins Romulus and Remus who, personifying Rome, gave new life and new impulse to Augusta Perusia.

The upper basin of the fountain is divided into panels without decorations, but its corners are embellished with 24 statues of saints, biblical personages and symbolic figures.

Irrespective of the precise symbolism of the various sculptures, what is so striking in the fountain is the extreme simplicity of its narrative scheme and the extraordinary synthetic capacity and incisiveness of its figural style, which give all the figures a particularly expressive and noble appearance.

*Piazza IV Novembre*
*Fontana Maggiore*

*Fontana Maggiore*

*To the side:*
*Statue symbolizing Perugia*
*(G. Pisano)*

*Below:*
*Water bearers (bronze statue*
*by Giovanni Pisano)*
*Some tiles representing the*
*months of the year,*
*February, May, June, July,*
*August, a Morality, October*

# The Cathedral

From the Piazza IV Novembre only the left side of the Cathedral can be seen. It is flanked by the large arcades of the 15th century **Loggia of Braccio Fortebraccio**. We may also note the fine geometric decoration in two colours of marble with which the lower storey of the Cathedral is veneered, the handsome bronze **statue of Pope Julius III** (1555: a distinguished work by Vincenzo Danti), the elegant 15th century **pulpit**, the two superimposed niches and the **Crucifix** protected behind glass, which has remained a symbol of the city's revolt against the Papal State during the "salt war".

The main façade of the Cathedral overlooks the adjacent Piazza Danti: it is incomplete with the exception of the elaborate baroque main entrance.

Begun in the 14th century in the gothic style, the Cathedral was not completed till the end of the 16th. The interior, consisting of a nave and aisles divided by tall gothic arches, is spacious in dimension, and contains works of art of considerable interest, of which we cite only the most important below.

On the entrance-wall of the church we may note a painting by G.A. Scaramuccia depicting the "Madonna and Child flanked by the Protector Saints of Perugia". To one side of the entrance is the fine sarcophagus of Andrea Baglioni sculpted by Urbano da Cortona in the mid-15th century.

A fine fresco of the "Madonna" by Giannicola di Paolo and another of "St. Bernardine,, by pupils of Perugino can be found against the piers of the nave.

**Right aisle:**
Starting from the entrance, we come first to the
– **Chapel of St. Bernardine**, enclosed behind magnificent railings. It contains one of Baroccio's finest paintings: his "Deposition from the Cross", dating to the late 16th century.
– **3rd Chapel**, also known as the Baptistery, because it contains the baptismal font and also a fresco of the "Baptism of Christ" by Domenico Bruschi, in a Renaissance architectural setting.
– **4th Chapel** (Chapel of the Sacrament); it is adorned with frescoes of the 16th and 18th century.

**Right transept**: it leads to the entrance to the **Chapel of St. Onophrius** with frescoes by Domenico Bruschi.

We then enter the **Sacristy**, whose walls present a wide range of 16th century frescoes, but whose architecture is in the Renaissance style.

From the Sacristy it is also possible to enter the **2 cloisters** annexed to the church which represent elegant examples of 15th century architecture and which have served, in the past, as the venues of papal Conclaves. Various archaeological remains are now housed in the cloisters.

**Sanctuary and apse**: particularly noteworthy are the magnificently carved and inlaid choir-stalls, a masterpiece by Giuliano da Maiano and Domenico del Tasso, and the wonderful Episcopal Throne.

**Left transept**: here we find the **Chapel of the Crucifix**, which derives its name from the wooden Crucifix placed over the altar (11th century). A painting of the "Martyrdom of St. Sebastian" by Orazio Alfani may also be noted.

**Left aisle**:
– "Pietà", a beautiful relief sculpted by Agostino di Duccio.

*Piazza IV Novembre and the Cathedral*
*To the side: Braccio Fortebraccio's loggias*

– "Gonfalone": this ceremonial standard placed over the altar was painted by Berto di Giovanni. The painting of the "Resurrection of Christ" is by Giannicola di Paolo.

– **Chapel of the Holy Ring**: facing the Chapel of St. Bernardine in the right aisle, it houses, behind a magnificent wrought-iron railing, a Tabernacle containing the betrothal-ring which, according to tradition, belonged to the Virgin Mary. The story goes that in 985 it was sold by a Jew to a jeweller in Chiusi, who was able to witness the resurrection of his dead son by merit of the holy relic. It was claimed to have worked many other miracles, so much so that the German friar Winter tried to gain possession of it and take it back to his homeland with him, but without succeeding. It was then that it was entrusted to the lord of Perugia Braccio Baglioni who, in consulation with the Priors of the city, took steps to ensure that it was worthily preserved in the Cathedral and venerated by its citizens. The painting over the altar of the chapel represents the "Betrothal between Mary and Joseph", a 19th century work by the painter Wicar.

Annexed to the Cathedral is

# The Cathedral Museum

The Cathedral Museum (**Museo dell'Opera del Duomo**) in entered through the Cathedral's second cloisters. It contains a rich collection of ancient documents and manuscripts, having been further enriched with the holdings of the Chapter Library. Also on display in its two rooms are a number of distinguished paintings, including interesting works by Luca Signorelli ("Madonna and Saints") and Bartolomeo Caporali ("Pietà"). Of the other artists represented in the collection we may mention Giannicola di Paolo, Andrea Vanni, pupils of Perugino, and Giovanni di Pietro (nicknamed Lo Spagna).

Opposite page:
Above, the façade of the Cathedral
of S. Lorenzo

Below:
The 15th c. pulpit from which San
Bernardino da Siena preached (left
side of the Cathedral);
Cloister of the Retory with 15th c.
portico

Above:
Inside of the Cathedral of S.
Lorenzo

To the side:
The venerated image of the
Madonna of Grace by Giannicola
di Paolo, pupil of the Perugino

# The Palazzo dei Priori

This magnificent civic building of great effect is undoubtedly one of the most significant medieval town-halls in Italy. It is striking for the powerful but at the same time elegant orchestration of its parts, its beautiful sequence of three-light mullioned windows decorating its exterior, like delicate lace-work, and its distinctive curvilinear façade facing onto the Corso Vannucci.

The Palazzo dei Priori was built between the late 13th and early 14th century; its architects were Giacomo di Servadio and Giovannello di Benvenuto. The part of the building facing onto the Corso was further prolonged in the 15th century.

The second façade of the building faces onto the Piazza IV Novembre. With its flight of steps leading up to the entrance, flanked by a loggia of three arcades, and its upper storey of elegant mullioned windows, it is noble and powerful in effect. The other wing of the Palazzo dei Priori, i.e. the longer one on the Corso Vannucci, is entered through a magnificently sculpted gothic portal surrounded by delicately carved floriated mouldings and twisted colonnettes.

## Interior

The Palazzo dei Priori is not only the Town-Hall of Perugia, but also houses the Municipal Library and National Gallery of Umbria. The various council rooms on the first floor can also be visited, notably the beautiful **Sala dei Notari**, a vaulted hall of noble dimensions and solemn appearance. The eight massive depressed arches on which its structure depends are completely frescoed with floral motifs, the coats of arms of former lords and dignitaries who have ruled over Perugia, and a series of biblical episodes taken from both the Old and New Testament; this monumental pictorial ensemble has commonly been attributed to pupils of Cavallini (14th century). The room became the seat of the Guild of Notaries (whence its name) in the 16th century; previously, the popular assemblies of the communal government of the city had been held in it.

*The Prior's Palace*
*and detail of the door*
*The Sala dei Notari*

# National Gallery of Umbria

Housed in the Palazzo dei Priori since the beginning of this century, the Gallery is of great importance for its review of Umbrian painting and the various influences to which it has been subjected, especially by Sienese and Florentine artists. The Gallery is mainly devoted to the period from the 13th to the 16th-17th century, and many artists of major repute are represented in it.

**Salone or Council Hall**: this is a large hall which played a memorable part in the medieval history of Perugia: it was here in fact that the General Council of the city was held. A number of frescoes removed from various churches in the town, and mainly dating to the 13th and 14th century, are now displayed in the hall. Particularly worth noting is a wooden "Crucifix" dating to the early years of the 13th century, undoubtedly the oldest work preserved in the Gallery.

**Room 1**: painting of the 13th century is represented here. The various artists displayed in this room include the so-called "Master of St. Francis", the anonymous master to whom a number of paintings have been attributed, some of them painted with the help of assistants; they include:
– "Crucifixion" (dated 1272)
– "Episodes from the Life of St. Anthony"
– panels of Saints Matthew and Francis
– "Episodes from the Life of Christ" (mainly attributable to pupils of the Master)
– "St. Clare, St. Francis, St. Michael and Gabriel".
Also on display in the room is a fine panel of the "Madonna and Child" by Duccio di Buoninsegna, notable for its delicacy and gentleness of expression.

**Room 2**: contains works by the Pisano brothers, including some pieces of sculpture or bas-reliefs removed from the Fontana Maggiore in Perugia, and some beautiful statuettes, highly expressive, carved by Arnolfo di Cambio. It may be noted that the room is incorporated within a tower of the palace.

**Room 3**: paintings of the first half of the 14th century. Of particular interest are a series of panels by Meo Guido da Siena (a polyptych and a series of representations of Saints) and an altarpiece of the "Madonna and Child Enthroned flanked by Saints" by Marino da Perugia.

**Room 4**: painting of the 14th century of the Umbrian and Tuscan schools. We may mention in this regard that the artists of Perugia, right down to the 15th century, were strongly influenced by pictorial developments in Tuscany, and especially by the Sienese masters, since they had left their masterpieces in nearby Assisi, whence a familiarity with their work had been disseminated to Perugia. Subsequently, it would be Florence, cradle of the great exponents of Renaissance painting, which would dictate the law in the artistic field.

Displayed in this room are works by a pupil of Meo da Siena, including a "Madonna and Child", "Episodes from the Life of Christ" and a "Maestà" (a typically Sienese theme). The painter Francesco da Rimini is represented by a panel of "St. Mary Magdalen".

The stained glass designed by Giovanni di Bonino is notable for the harmony and balance of its composition.

*Hall*
*"Madonna with Child" - Duccio di Buoninsegna*

*On the opposite page:*
*"Crucifix" - Maestro di San Francesco, XIII c.*

**Room 5**: painting of Sienese masters of the 14th and 15th century. They include, in particular, a fine series of paintings by Taddeo di Bartolo:
- "Annunciation"
- "Pentecost"
- "St. Peter and St. Paul"
- "Madonna and Child"
- allegories of "Lust, Pride and Avarice vanquished by St. Francis". The room also contains works by Lippo Vanni ("Madonna and Child"), Nicolò di Buanaccorso ("Christ on the Cross") and Andrea and Domenico di Bartolo.

**Room 6**: Gothic painting
- "Madonna and Child", an exquisite panel of great charm and delicacy by Gentile da Fabriano, one of the most significant exponents of the gothic style in painting in Italy.
- "Madonna and Child" by Ottaviano Nelli, one of the best known and most active Umbrian artists of the earlier 15th century.
- panels by Lello da Velletri, Bicci di Lorenzo, Mariotto di Nardo and others.

Some works of sculpture are also displayed in this room.

**Room 7**: contains some of the most important of the paintings held by the National Gallery of Umbria: the mere names of the artists in questions are enough to demonstrate their value:
- "Madonna and Child with Saints and Angels" by Fra Angelico (panel of the 1st half of the 15th century).
- "Madonna and Child flanked by Saints, with the Annunciation above": a magnificent polyptych and predella (with little scenes from the lives of St. Francis, St. Anthony and St. Elizabeth) by the great 15th century master Piero della Francesca.
- "The Scourging of Christ", a bronze sculpture by Francesco di Giorgio Martini.
- "Madonna and Child" by Benozzo Gozzoli

**Room 8**: Umbrian painting
Works by Niccolò Alunno, Giovanni Boccati and Matteo di Gualdo are displayed in this room.

**Room 9**: a room devoted to the work of the Perugian artist Benedetto Bonfigli (1454-96). The various panels by Bonfigli on display include:
- "Annunciation"
- "Madonna and Child"
- "Adoration of the Magi".

**Room 10**: painting of the 15th century. Paintings by Girolamo da Cremona, Mariano D'Antonio Nutoli, Antoniazzo da Romano and other minor Renaissance masters are contained in this room.

**Room 11**: on display in this room are works by Fiorenzo di Lorenzo and Domenico Caporali, two Perugian artists who lived between the late 15th and early 16th century.

**Room 12**: works by Fiorenzo di Lorenzo and Pietro Vannucci, better known as Perugino. The latter, after having spent some time in Florence and been subjected to masters like Verrocchio and Piero della Francesca and after having worked in Rome, settled in Perugia, and it was there that he painted some of his greatest masterpieces (hence the nickname by which he is now known is derived from the city), especially his frescoes in the Collegio del Cambio (see below).

In this gallery Perugino is represented by:
- "The Adoration of the Magi"
- "Pietà"

Also worth noting in this room are some fine enamelled terracottas produced by artists belonging to the school of the Della Robbia.

*National Gallery of Umbria*
*"Christ's Deposition from the Cross",*
*Romanesque Art in Central Italy first half*
*of the XIII c.*
*"Christ dead" attributed to Raffaello*

*On the next page:*
*Polyptych - Piero della Francesca (1406-1492)*

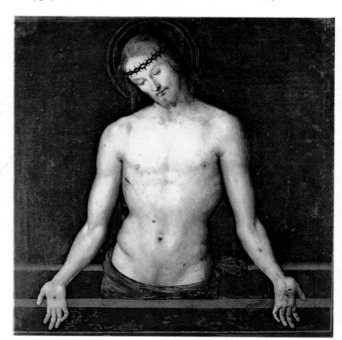

**Room 14**: a work of great distinction is displayed in this room: namely, the **gonfalone** or church-banner of St. Bernardine, painted for processions in honour of the Saint. It was painted by Perugino, Pinturicchio and pupils of the former. It undoubtedly represents one of the greatest expressions of Umbrian art of the period.

**Room 15**: paintings by Perugino and Pinturicchio. Among the works of the former we may mention:
– a predella with "Scenes from the life of Jesus"
– the so-called "Madonna della Consolazione"
– "Dead Christ"
– "Madonna and Child with Saints"
Pinturicchio's works include:
– "Pietà and Saints"
– "Madonna and Child with Saints".

**Room 16**: in this small room is displayed an exquisitely painted "Pietà" by Piero di Cosimo.

**Room 17**: contains paintings by Bernardino di Mariotto and other Perugian artists.

**Room 18**: the artist best represented in this room is Giannicola di Paolo, but panels by Spagna and his imitators are also on view.

**Room 19**: contained in this room are especially works by Berto di Giovanni (his "St. John" and "Episodes from the Life of St. John"), as well as altarpieces by Sibaldo Ibi and Eusebio di San Giorgio ("Madonna and Child", "Adoration of the Magi", "Madonna and Child between St. Benedict and St. John").

**Room 20**: this room is devoted to works by followers of Perugino and Raphael. They include Domenico Alfani, who is represented by various panels of the "Madonna and Child with Saints", an "Adoration of the Magi" and a representation of "God the Father with Angels", which formed part of an altarpiece by Raphael. The other artists on display include Orazio di Domenico Alfani of whom many paintings are preserved.

**Room 21**: Umbrian painting of the 16th century. The painters represented in this room include Dono Doni (a native of Assisi), whose "Nativity of Mary" is on view, Benedetto Nucci and others.

**Room 22**: not really a room, but a long corridor flanked by various cabinets in which are displayed a series of reliquaries and precious liturgical objects such as chalices, crosiers, Crucifixes, and other church furnishings of great value.

**Room 23**: particularly splendid is the decoration of this room which at one time served as the Chapel of the Palazzo dei Priori. Its walls are decorated with a series of frescoes in large part painted by Bendetto Bonfigli and depicting "Scenes from the Life of St. Louis of Toulouse", set against the background of the city of Perugia, whose appearance at the time is faithfully reproduced. Also of interest are the finely-carved choir-stalls and an urn which was used as a ballot box during elections at the time when Perugia was a city-state.

**Room 24**: dedicated to Agostino di Duccio, a distinguished Florentine sculptor of the 15th century. He is represented here by various statues or fragments of statues (the "Madonna and Child" is particularly lovely) which once adorned churches in Perugia and in particular a no longer extant Oratorio situated on the Via della Maestà delle Volte.

*National Gallery of Umbria*
*"Madonna of Consolation called of the Beaten" Pietro Perugino (1445-1523)*
*"Madonna with Child and Saints" Pietro Perugino (1445-1523)*
*Opposite page:*
*Central part of the Polyptych of the Dominicans-Beato Angelico*

*National Gallery of Umbria*
*"Madonna with Child and Saints"*
*Domenico di Bartolo (1400-1447)*

*"Madonna with Child and Saints" Benozzo Gozzoli (1420-1497)*

*Opposite page: "The Adoration of the Magi" - Pietro Perugino (1445-1523)*

## The Sala del Collegio della Mercanzia

The seat of the Guild of Merchants during the communal period, this is a magnificent chamber of late-gothic appearance. It is completely veneered in carved and inlaid wood and has seats running along the walls.

Documents and illuminated books of the period are preserved in the annexed Archive.

A short distance ahead we come to

# The Collegio del Cambio

This was the old chamber of commerce and exchange, and today constitutes a real jewel of Umbrian Renaissance art thanks to the magnificent frescoes and other decorations that adorn its walls. On passing through the **vestibule** with baroque decorations by Zuccari, we enter the **Audience Hall**, a room of wonderful effect.

The lower part of its walls is veneered with elegantly carved and inlaid wood panelling, with seats, the tribunal or judicial throne and a beautifully carved money-changers' bench (by Domenico del Tasso). Also noteworthy is a fine statue of "Justice" by Benedetto da Maiano.

The upper part of the walls and the vaulted ceiling are completely covered with frescoes, which undoubtedly represent the masterpiece of Pietro Vannucci better known as Perugino and several painters belonging to his school.

On the end wall (opposite the entrance) are depicted:
– "The Transfiguration of Christ"
– "The Birth of Christ"
On the wall to its right we see:
– "Glory of God" (above) and groups of "Prophets" (Isaiah, Moses, Daniel, David, Jeremiah, Solomon) and "Sibyls" (Erythrean, Persian, Cumaean, Libyan, Tiburtine and Delphian sibyls). The 3rd Prophet seems to be a portrait of the young Raphael, who was a pupil of Perugino and who is thought by art historians to have been one of the master's assistants in the execution of these frescoes.

On the wall to the left:
– Allegorical representations of "Fortitude" and "Temperance" (above)
– below: personages from ancient history who distinguished themselves by these virtues (Lucius Sicinius, Leonidas, Horatius Cocles, Scipio, Pericles and Cincinnatus)
– Allegorical representations of "Prudence" and "Justice" (above)
– below: personages from ancient history who distinguished themselves by these virtues (Fabius Maximus, Socrates, Numa Pompilius, Furius Camillus, Pittacus and Trajan).

On the pillar between the arches dividing the wall we may note a self-portrait of Perugino.

A door leads into the adjacent **Chapel**: its pictorial decoration was the work of Giannicola di Paolo.

*Collegio del Cambio*
*Page from a miniature code of the XIV c.*
*Pietro Vannucci called il Perugino (1445-1523) –*
*"a self portrait"*
*Opposite page:*
*Collegio della Mercanzia*
*Collegio del Cambio– Hall of Audience*

# The Rocca Paolina
## Via Bagliona

We find ourselves confronted by an extraordinary sequence of houses and little streets belonging to the ancient medieval quarter which was incorporated by Pope Paul III in the fortress – the Rocca Paolina – he built over it, once the popular revolt known as the "salt war" had been quelled and the **signoria** of the Baglioni who resided here, defeated. Having established his own authority in the city, the Farnese Pope then erected, as a symbol of it, the fortress named after him.

Wonder and awe are the emotions felt by the visitor on being confronted by this slice of the past, made all the more picturesque and unforgettable by the silence with which it is imbued. And the flickering lamps that accompany the route between the old buildings of this submerged world heighten still more the sense of antiquity. Everything, in these underground houses, seems to have remained unchanged, frozen in time, and the fortress built round the old houses of the Baglioni seems to stand guard over them to protect them against the ravages of time.

The Via Bagliona skirts houses and towers of the 14th and 16th century, intersecting streets of that old quarter and reveating, at every corner, vivid glimpses into the past, into a period of exceptional interest in the history of Perugia. Above all, it reveals, to the attentive and astonished eye of the visitor, an atmosphere charged with historical memory and emotion. A vanished world springs to life: the old buildings with their silent windows, the remains of ancient towers – no less than 25 stood here –, the surviving terracotta or majolica pavements, the many well-heads, the little shops, the arches flung over the streets, the cellars and kitchens.

Descending the last stretch of moving staircase inside the Rocca Paolina, we may see the remains of the pitch once used for an ancient ballgame (the "Gioco del Pallone"): the wooden stadium that once delimited it has completely vanished, but we can see some ruins in stone that formed part of it, situated abutting onto a fortified corridor (or passage-way) of the Rocca Paolina itself.

## The Porta Marzia

A wonderful ancient town-gate (not easily datable, but probably attributable to the 2nd or 1st century B.C.). It was incorporated by the architect Antonio da Sangallo the Younger in the walls of the Fortress – and here the tall and massive external bastions of the Rocca Paolina can clearly be seen – after having dismantled and reassembled it in a slightly different position than before.

*Porta Marzia and Lomellina fountain*
*Via Ritorta - a mediaeval street*

*Opposite page:*
*Rocca Paolina, the guard room (above)*
*Via Bagliona (below)*

# The Piazza Matteotti

The Piazza Matteotti is characterized by ancient buildings with a robust but elegant appearance. First we may note the **church of the Gesù** (16th century) with an interior decorated with frescoes and a beautiful ceiling, and two fine **Oratories**. Just beyond is the entrance to a **Loggia** and to the Market, an area which rests on the tall buttresses constructed to counteract the steep gradient of the hill on which the city stands and to support the piazza itself.

We then observe the handsome **Palace of the Captain of the People**. It was built in the 15th century by Gasparino di Antonio and Leone di Matteo. It is entered through an elegant round-arched portal adorned with a statue of "Justice" and two griffins, emblems of the city. Above is a second storey pierced by beautiful two-light mullioned windows surmounted by a pronounced entablature. The loggia is the one from which public proclamations were made.

Next to it stands the **Palazzo dell'Universita**, so called because it was the former seat of the University. It has a series of deep gothic arches on the ground floor and an order of cruciform (Guelph cross) windows on the upper floor.

**THE VIA MAESTÀ DELLE VOLTE**. A short but scenic street full of picturesque views and majestic historical buildings. After the little church of the same name – with fine frescoes by Pomarancio inside – we come to a series of large arches which rest on the buildings to the side of the street and open up memorable views of the medieval houses and little streets descending to the lower part of the city.

# The Via dei Priori

This scenic street descends between ancient buildings, intersected by alleyways and little piazzas rich in fascination and interest. First we come to the **church of Sant'Agata**, to the left of the Via dei Priori and at the beginning of the street named after the church. This is an ancient 13th century building with a simple façade, adorned by a handsome round-arched portal decorated with colonnettes. The interior of the church substantially retains its original Romanesque-Gothic plan, as well as some remains of frescoes of the period.

Further ahead, in the Piazza B. Ferri, is the **church of San Filippo Neri**, raised over a broad flight of stairs.

We continue down the Via dei Priori, noting the intriquing succession of views opened up by the many little alleys whose names are equally picturesque (a feature characteristic of a large part of the streets of Perugia). By taking the Via della Cupa we can reach the **Porta della Mandorla**, another gateway in the town walls (of Etruscan origin but transformed in the medieval period), after passing the **Collegio della Sapienza** and the **church of the Annunziata**.

On the Via Deliziosa, another side street leading off from the Via dei Priori, we may find the house traditionally identified as that lived in by the artist Perugino.

Continuing down the Via dei Priori itself, we pass the **churches of Santi Stefano e Valentina** and **Santa Teresa**, followed by the superb medieval tower known as the **Torre degli Sciri** (12th century). We then enter the small but picturesque Piazza della Madonna della Luce, on which are situated the **church of the Madonna della Luce** (16th century), the **Arch of San Luca** and the **church of the Madonna di San Luca**.

Finally we come to the large and spacious Piazza San Francesco. Looking onto the square are the **church of San Francesco** (13th in origin, but substantially remodelled), the **Convent of San Francesco** (seat of the Academy of Fine Arts), and the **Chapel of the Confraternity of the Holy Conception**. This latter contains works of great interest, such as Bonfigli's painting of the "Madonna della Mercede", various tombs of illustrious personages, the reliquary containing one of the thorns from the cross of Christ and a fine 14th century altar. Also of interest is the decoration of geometric motifs covering part of the wall surfaces.

*Palace of the Captain of the People*

*Via Maestà delle Volte*
*Church of San Francesco al Prato*
*Sciri Tower, XIII c.*

# Church of San Bernardino

A masterpiece of architecture by the Florentine sculptor Agostino di Duccio (15th century). Erected over the site where St. Bernardine had preached, it is a wonderful example of renaissance art. The magnificently decorated façade consists of a large central arch surmounted by a tympanum and flanked by two lateral parts slightly splayed towards the top; this architectural device is aimed at compensating for and correcting the optical effect which, according to the laws of perspective, would otherwise lead to a narrowing of the surfaces towards the top of the façade. The whole façade is embellished with sculptures and bas-reliefs which are among the finest of the period. The polychrome effect produced by the interplay of differently coloured marbles and terracotta is also extremely pleasing.

Facing onto the Piazza Fortebraccio is the **Palazzo Gallenga Stuart**, a notable 18th century building which is now the seat of the **Università per Stranieri** (Foreigners' University), founded at the beginning of this century with the aim of diffusing Italian culture abroad; it remains the only study centre for foreigners at the university level in Italy.

The **Etruscan Arch** or **Arch of Augustus**: an ancient town-gate. We are here faced by one of the most striking and impressive buildings of antiquity: its compact and imposing architectural structure, made all the more austere and solid by the sombre colour of its masonry, its archway framed by massive projecting buttresses incorporated in the ancient circuit of walls, bear eloquent witness to the grandeur and importance of Perugia in antiquity.

The arch, which is Etruscan in origin (3rd century B.C.), was restored by the Romans in the 1st century B.C., as part of Octavian's reconstruction of the city which then assumed (in his honour) the name of **Augusta Perusia**: a name which can be read in the imperial inscription over the arch. The gateway consists of a single tall arch built of massive blocks of ashlared masonry. Above it is an attic decorated with an ornamental band of sculptured shields, with a blind arch above it.

The loggia placed over one of the projecting buttresses that flank the monument and the fountain below were added in the 16th century.

From the Arch of Augustus, by following the Via Battisti which runs between the arch itself and the Palazzo Gallenga, we can reach the Piazza Morlacchi after skirting a magnificent stretch of the Etruscan walls in which various buildings are also incorporated. This **circuit of walls** built of large squared blocks runs round a long stretch of the perimeter of Perugia, and surrounds the upper part of the city: it extends from the Porta Marzia to the Porta Sant'Ercolano; then it rises to the Porta Sole, before descending again to the Arch of Augustus along the Via delle Prome; it then reascends along the aforementioned Via Battisti, and then continues towards the Piazza San Francesco and, beyond that, the Piazzale della Cupa.

*St. Bernardino Oratorium*
*The Etruscan Arch*

*Opposite page:*
*Palazzo Gallenga (1754) seat of the*
*Italian University for Foreigners*
*Morlacchi Municipal Theatre - 1788*

# The Church of San Domenico

A large and imposing building that dominates the panorama of Perugia, it is incomplete in its external cladding. Dating to the 14th century, the church was in large part reconstructed by the architect Maderno in the 17th, following the collapse of much of the building. Recent restoration has, however, permitted the recuperation of part of its gothic structure, especially that of its 4th Chapel in the Right Aisle, in which the beautiful pictorial **decoration by Agostino di Duccio** has also remained intact.

A number of works of art of considerable value are preserved in the church: apart from the aforementioned frescoes, we should especially note the elegantly inlaid wooden **choir-stalls** (15th century), the large and wonderful stained-glass window in the apse dating to the Early Renaissance period, the 14th century frescoes which decorate some of the walls of the chapels and, in particular, the beautiful **monument to Pope Benedict XI** in the left transept. This wonderful example of gothic funerary art is of uncertain attribution (the names of the Pisano, Lorenzo Maitani and Arnolfo di Cambio have all been proposed). It is in the shape of a tabernacle: above the recumbent figure of the Pope (who died in 1304) rises a lofty canopy borne by spiral columns. The tomb is decorated with mosaics and sculptural groups.

## The National Archaeological Museum of Umbria

This is an archaeological collection of major importance, notable for the richness of its holdings and the wide-ranging panorama it provides of the ancient civilizations present not only in Umbrian territory but in large part of Central Italy.

It currently consists of two sections: firstly, an Etruscan-Roman section assembled at the end of the 18th century thanks to the Friggeri bequest and successively enriched with other donations and finds; and secondly, a prehistoric section which was combined with the former in c. 1950, when it was decided to transfer the artefacts previously housed in the Palazzo Donini to the Museum's present premises at San Domenico.

On entering the former convent of San Domenico, we find ourselves in the Large Cloisters, erected in the Renaissance style by the architect Mansueti. Here and in the eleven rooms of the ground floor is distributed the

## Etruscan-Roman Section

The collection comprises finds of every type ranging in date from the 6th century B.C. to the 2nd century A.D., and for the most part found in the territory of Umbria, and that of Perugia in particular, but also in various areas of Latium and the Marche. This extensive area, and especially Perugia itself, was for a long time under Etruscan domination, and this explains the wealth of artefacts and finds referable to Etruscan civilization on diplay in the Museum. This civilization is in fact comprehensively represented in all its aspects and also in the various phases which characterized the development of its social and artistic life, from the archaic period to that of its maximum maturity.

The collection of finds of the Roman period is also very rich. The Roman antiquities mainly come from Umbrian territory, and in particular from the excavations of Carsulae, Spoleto and Perugia.

The Etruscan-Roman Section comprises funerary urns, cippi, inscriptions, weapons and tomb-furniture, vases of every type, statues and architectural fragments, jewellery, brooches and other ornaments, and remains of decorations. They come from the excavations of Farfa in Lazio, Cetona, Bettona, Assisi and Corciano, and from the Perugian cemeteries of Santa Giuliana, Monteluce and Frontone.

*Church of San Domenico*
*- the main cloister*

*Basilica of San Domenico*
*- Benedetto XI's sepulchre*

*Church of San Domenico*
*- large coloured window*

## Prehistoric Section

The Prehistoric Section is displayed on the convent's upper floor. Of the greatest interest, it comprises artefacts recovered from excavations carried out throughout Central Italy, and ranging in date from the Palaeolithic (Stone Age) to the Bronze and Iron Ages. The Museum thus provides significant documentation on the presence of prehistoric man in these territories, and especially the gradual but continuous development in the techniques of working the various materials. In going through the various rooms and observing the objects mounted and catalogued in the display-cases, we are enabled to follow the successive stages in the prehistory of man and trace the evolution of the techniques invented and used by him to better respond to his own needs and those of the moment.

We begin with the first rudimentary stone tools, offensive weapons, scrapers and pointed implements made from roughly flaked flint (we are in the Early Palaeolithic period). Later, the same tools assume greater refinement and efficiency; they are dressed and polished more carefully, and flaked more expertly to produce sharper cutting edges. Eventually the Stone Age gave way to the Neolithic and to the emergence not only of more elaborate artefacts, but of a whole range of new tools, invented in response to the development of new economic systems, notably agriculture. At the same time, the increasing wealth generated by farming is reflected in the appearance of the first jewels and personal adornments.

Soom of the rooms in this section, and more precisely Rooms 6, 7 and 8, display the material subdivided according to the zones in which the excavations were carried out: they are mainly sites in Umbria such as Norcia, Parrano, and San Martino in Colle. And the artefacts in question dating to the Palaeolithic and Neolithic in many cases testify not only to the state of isolation of these groups of primitive men (many of the scrapers, axe-heads and pointed flint tools in fact date to the very early Stone Age), but also to the surprising analogies that can be identified between groups living at considerable distances between each other.

The subsequent Bronze and Iron Ages are amply documented in the so-called **Salone dei Metalli**: here the artefacts on display range from the first objects in copper made by rudimentary founding techniques, to sophisticately cast implements in bronze and iron. The weapons both of offensive and defensive type, the household utensils and the ornamental objects are continuously refined in technique, and assume ever more elaborate, variegated and decorative shapes. The display-cases contain artefacts and implements of the most varied kind; some of them are chance finds, others yielded by excavations conducted throughout Central Italy. Particularly significant is the collection of finds from Cetona, a hill-town on the border between Umbria and Tuscany which was inhabited in prehistoric times and remarkable for its flourishing Bronze and Iron Age culture in the 2nd millennium B.C.

The former Convent of San Domenico also contains the premises of the **STATE ARCHIVES**, justly famous not only for the wealth and value of the historical documents it comprises, but also for its modern conservation techniques and advanced archival facilities.

*National Archaeological Museum of Umbria*
*The cïppus (memorial stone) of Perugia*

*Opposite page:*
*Finely engraved Etruscan mirror*
*Greek crater found in an Etruscan tomb*
*Showcase with bronze statuettes - Etruscan age*

# The Church of San Pietro

This is another of the city's illustrious monuments. Its construction was initiated by the Perugian monk Pietro Vincioli in the 10th century. It is flanked by a beautiful bell-tower designed by Rossellino in the 15th century; a superb view of it can be had from inside the courtyard in front of the church.

The interior of San Pietro, a basilica consisting of a nave, aisles and transept with a richly gilded ceiling supported by antique columns, is striking both for its interesting architectural structure and the richness of the works of art it contains.

**Nave:**

It is delimited by magnificent columns and topped by an elegant ceiling. According to tradition, the 2nd column to the left was miraculously supported by St. Pietro when it was about to fall down. Above the nave are a series of large paintings by the Perugian artist Vassillacchi (16th century) depicting "**Scenes from the Life of Christ**".

The entrance-wall of the church is decorated with another large picture by Vassillacchi reproducing the "Genealogical Tree of the Benedictine Order", and frescoes by Orazio Alfani and L. Cungi.

(The works listed below are generally situated over the altars along the aisles, and in the spaces between them).

**Left Aisle**:

– 1st space: "Episodes from the Lives of St. Maurus and St. Placidus"

– 2nd space: "Pietà" by Perugino

– 2nd altar: "Crucifix"

– 3rd space: "Annunciation", a reproduction of a painting by Raphael

– 3rd altar: "Assumption of Mary" by Domenico Alfani

– 4th space: "The Magi" by Eusebio da San Giorgio

Chapel of the Sacrament: it contains paintings by Vasari and local Perugian artists.

– 5th space: "Judith" by Sassoferrato

Ranieri Chapel: it was designed by Francesco di Guido; the frescoes in the vault are by Annibale Brugnoli. Also noteworthy is the fine painting by Guido Reni.

– 6th space: "Deposition from the Cross", a work by Sassoferrato reproducing a painting by Raphael.

Vibi Chapel: also built by Francesco di Guido, it contains paintings by Caporali, Giannicola di Paolo and others. Of particular note is the beautiful marble tabernacle sculpted by Mino da Fiesole.

– Facing the two chapels: "St. Peter" and "St. Paul", important works by the 17th century master Guercino

– 7th space: "Pietà between Saints", perhaps by Benedetto Bonfigli.

**Apse**:

The High Altar is striking. It was erected in the later 16th century by V. Martelli, who conceived it as a tabernacle sumptuously decorated with precious marbles and other rare stones to provide a worthy monument for the body of the canonized monk who had built the church, Pietro Vincioli.

*Church of San Pietro -*
*inside*
*Santa Francesca Romana*
*by Michelangelo Merisi*
*The Bell-Tower*

Yet the most striking work in the apse are the magnificent walnut **choir-stalls**, admirably carved and inlaid by Stefano da Bergamo (1535), and rightly regarded by art historians as the finest of their kind in Italy, due to the extraordinary intricacy and delicacy of their intarsias.

Magnificent panoramic views over the Tiber valley can be enjoyed from the doors at the back of the apse. The framed signature of the Italian poet Giosuè Carducci may be noted; he visited the church and stopped here to enjoy the view that opened up before him.

Proceeding from the apse to the right aisle, we come first of all to the entrance to the **Sacristy**. Various works of art of some interest are displayed here, including the four small half-figure panels of saints ("Saints Placido, Ercolano, Peter Abbot and Costanzo") painted by Perugino; and the "Holy Family" by Parmigianino, a painting of great charm and elegance in which the eyes of the Virgin seem constantly to be fixed on the observer, no matter how often he changes position. Also noteworthy is a painting by Caravaggio: his "Saint Francesca Romana". The fine series of 16th century miniatures by the Boccardi family should also be noted.

**Right Aisle**:
– Above the entrance to the Sacristy: pictures of "Saints", copies by Sassoferrato from paintings by Perugino
    – 1st space: "The Risen Christ" by Orazio Alfani
    – Opposite: "The Madonna as a Child" by Cerrini
    – Above the door: "Madonna and Child with Saints" by Bonifacio Veronese
    – Opposite: "Pietà", attributed to the school of Sebastiano del Piombo
    – 2nd space: "Samson" by Francesco Perrier
    – Chapel of St. Joseph: it contains works by imitators of Raphael and Andrea Del Sarto.
    – 3rd space: "St. Gregory the Great in procession" by Ventura Salimbeni
    – 1st altar: "St. Benedict handing over the Rule of his Order to his Monks", a painting by Eusebio di San Giorgio
    – 4th space: "David" by Ventura Salimbeni
    – 6th space: "Assumption of Mary" by Orazio Alfani
    – 7th space: "Madonna and Child with Saints" by Eusebio da San Giorgio.

The **church of Santa Giuliana**, erected in the mid-13th century. Its exterior is elegant, characterized by contrastingly coloured marbles that form a decoration of geometric motis. The interior of the church is also of some interest, containing as it does a cycle of frescoes attributed to a pupil of Cimabue, of which the scene of the "Last Supper" is particularly striking.

The adjacent Military Hospital now occupies the ancient **Convent of Santa Giuliana**, which retains the beautiful 14th century architecture of some of its rooms and especially an elegant and harmonious Cloister.

The **church of Sant'Ercolano**. Particularly beautiful is the siting of this church which rises, proudly and elegantly, on top of a fine stairway. Polygonal in plan, its exterior is animated by delicate hanging arches and large blind arcades. Inside, it retains its original structure dating to the 13th-14th century, though its decoration is later. The church now houses the Shrine to the Fallen. It was erected on the site on which St. Ercolano, Bishop of Perugia, was martyred on the orders of Totila the Goth in the 6th century; he later became patron saint of the city together with St. Costanzo.

The **church of Sant'Angelo**. This is architecturally of the greatest interest and undoubtedly one of the most important monuments in the city. In fact, it is one of the best preserved Early Christian churches to come down to us. Erected in the 6th century, probably over a pre-existing Roman building, it has a circular structure with 16 antique columns in the interior, which is also circular. The columns are arranged in an inner circle, with an ambulatory around them, and support the vaulted roof. The church is of extreme simplicity, but is most striking.

Continuing beyond this church, we come, at the end of the Via Garibaldi, to the Porta Sant'Angelo, a town-gate erected by Lorenzo Maitani in the 14th century, and opened in the city's outer circuit of walls, i.e. the walls built in the Middle Ages.

The **church of Santa Maria di Monteluce**. Originally built in the 14th century, the church has been subjected to several alterations and restorations. Its portal is 15th century, leading into the interior where part of the original structure can be seen, as well as a gothic altar and a fine marble tabernacle. Of considerable interest are the frescoes by Fiorenzo di Lorenzo and those of the Umbrian school that decorate the walls of the Oratory adjoining the church.

*Church of Sant'Angelo*

*Church of Monteluce*
*Church of Sant'Ercolano*
*Church of Santa Giuliana - XIV c.*
*Cloister and bell tower*

# The "Città della Domenica"

This is an extensive fun-fair and amusement park laid out for the entertainment of children and young people: a park not dissimilar, in some respects, to the more famous Disneyland in the U.S.A. Games of every time, miniature trains which run along the little streets of the hill on which the park is laid out, reconstructions of castels and historic houses, as well as of personages from the fairy-stories and adventure-stories best loved by children, a small but interesting zoological garden, a museum and reconstructions of historic weapons or modern missiles: these are some of the main features of this city in miniature (the "City of Sunday" as its name means in English) which occupies the upper slopes of a hill rising close to the Cortona state highway in the environs of Perugia.

# The Hypogeum of the Volumnii

This is one of the finest and most complete Etruscan mausolea to have come down to us. Various other underground tombs have been found in the environs of the city, such as those of San Manno, the one by the Villa Sperandio and the one close to Bettona. But this is, without a doubt, the most important and the best known.

The Hypogeum is an underground tomb containing the mortal remains of a noble Etruscan family, that of the Volumnii. Hewn into the soft volcanic rock, it is laid out on a plan similar to that of the typical Roman house (we may note the atrium, the tablinum and the cubicula). This attests both to the prestige the family enjoyed, and the importance that Etruscan civilization attributed to the life of the hereafter. The Etruscans paid the greatest consideration to the link – a very real one they thought – between life on earth and life beyond the tomb: indeed, the latter was regarded as an indissoluble continuation of the former and, just for this reason, the deceased wished to recreate, in his tomb, the domestic environment that had been familiar to him and to assemble together within it everything that had been most dear to him.

In the various rooms into which the tomb is divided, grouped round an oblong central space, are seven magnificent funerary urns which contained the ashes of members of the Volumnii family.

The rooms preceding the Hypogeum, built in modern times, contain a display of various artefacts recovered during excavations at other sites in the environs of Perugia.

*Cinerary urn of Auruntus Volumnius of Aulo (2nd century B.C.).*

# Assisi

Assisi, the Umbrian town which was for centuries been known throughout the world as the hometown of Sain Francis and as a recognised centre of Christianity, has become, thanks to the inspiring example of the life and work of the great saint of Assisi and the whole vast movement of ideas and feelings that has sprung up around him and his order, the symbol of peace in the world. It has become its ideal centre and propulsor, the point of aggregation of the aspirations of all men and women of conscience, be they Catholics or non-Catholics, believers or atheists, who strongly believe in and wish to foster the fundamental and inalienable values of the co-existence of all mankind.

For years now, this wonderful Umbrian town has been the chosen venue of the march for peace organized at the regional and international level, and a whole series of events, meetings and conferences dedicated to the same theme. From Assisi, too, have been launched a series of universal messages and appeals addressed to every corner of the earth and aimed at finding a solution to the major problems that afflict the world's peoples.

It was at Assisi, moreover, in the square facing the Basilica of St. Francis, that a truly exceptional meeting took place, and one that was destined to become historic: the highest representatives of all the most representative religions in every part of the world, ranging from those with the widest diffusion such as Catholicism and Islam to those which have a numerically more restricted following but which have been inseparably linked for millennia with the civilization of the various peoples, met togheter, transcending the particular claims of their own faiths in order to recognise and confirm the universal concept of divinity and, more especially, the absolute value of peace as the irreplaceable postulate for co-existence and for the intrinsic dignity of all peoples.

Assisi, therefore, already made so mystical, so rich in spirituality, so universal by her greatest son who turned her, then as now, into a beacon of religious revival and deep Christian conviction based on simplicity and purity of soul, still continues today to perform this role which Saint Francis embodied and inculcated as the foundation of a humanity that believes in the values of brotherly love between men and peoples.

The town, now more than ever, seems to correspond to the concept that Dante Alighieri wished to see inherent in its very name: for the great poet, in fact, Assisi meant "**Ascesi**", meaning the rising of the sun in the east, because it was just in this town that the man had been born, the sun risen – St. Francis, in other words – who was destined to cast his light over the whole of mankind.

Today we, recurring to the happy image of Dante, can with some justice affirm that Assisi, by continuing to uphold and promote the tradition which has made her a protagonist of history and Christianity, is in the process of becoming the dawn of a new humanity.

# Historical and artistic background

Apart from the legends concerning its remote past and precisely its origins, we know for sure that Assisi was one of the ancient Umbrian centres, often fighting against the nearby Etruscan towns, with which, however, it joined forces in order to face the Roman invasion. It was then a Roman municipium named Asisium. During this period it developed considerably as far as economy and public works were concerned. Even nowadays the beautiful and well kept Temple of Minerva, now transformed into a church, the ruins of the Amphitheatre and of the Theatre, and a Roman cistern bear witness to that flourishing period. Asisium was also the homeland of the Latin poet Propertius.

After the fall of the Roman Empire, the town went through various vicissitudes, till it was annexed to the Longobard Dukedom of Spoleto.

At the beginning of the 11th century Assisi became a Free Town. It had to fight, however, against the nearby Perugia, but at the end they both signed a treaty of peace. It was in this period (1182) that Giovanni di Bernardone (later St. Francis) was born. He would influence the life itself of the town not only from a religious point of view, but also and mainly as far as art and culture were concerned. It's enough to consider not only the churches and the religious buildings that would be built – first of all, the Basilica of St. Francis – but also all the artists (mainly Giotto), who would adorn the church with their pictorial masterpieces characterizing most of the art of that time (we shall speak later about the developments and features of this important aspect of the matter). Thanks to the cultural revival promoted by the Franciscan movement, many buildings and churches rose in this period, while many others were restored, transformed and enlarged. Besides the Basilica of St. Francis, the church of St. Clare was built, while the churches of St. Ruphinus and St. Peter were made even more beautiful. The palace of the People's Captain, that of Mt. Frumentario and some gates were built at that time. Apart from Cimabue and Giotto, the Master of St. Francis' and that of St. Clare's, Giunta Pisano and Pietro Lorenzetti were active in the painting field.

After a period of quiet mainly because it had made its peace with Perugia, during the Renaissance Assisi was ruled by various Lords, whose domination was characterized by bloody fights against the nearby towns causing terrible ransacks and devastations.

During that period, however, other fine palaces and fountains were built, while Andrea and Tiberio of Assisi were active in the painting field. After that period, the most important work of art is the Basilica of St. Mary of the Angels, whose architect was Galeazzo Alessi, who would work also at the restoration of the interior of St. Ruphinus' Cathedral. The creative zeal, however, that had characterized the preceding centuries, diminished.

At the beginning of the 16th century, the most tormented age of Assisi's history ended. It was annexed to the Pontifical State, under which it would remain without any particular problem, till it was annexed to the Kingdom of Italy (1860).

From that time on, its history has been practically that of the Italian State.

# The Basilica of St. Francis and the Sacred Convent

Our eyes sweep a wide but peaceful, silent, deeply religious space, though crowded with numberless tourists. We are surprised at that series of arcades situated along the side of the square. It is a solitary, simple and quiet portico, covered with a very simple roof. It was built in the 15th century and meant to house all the pilgrims and sick people coming from all parts of Italy. Its extremely simple structure helps to create that mystical and pure atmosphere so typical of the Franciscan movement and its Founder and anticipates the simple architectural lines of the Basilica.

At the end of the square there is the entrance to the **SACRED CONVENT**, easily recognizable thanks to its elegant and simple portal with a double corona set in a very simple façade, apart from the fine bi-coloured underlining of the stone creating some longitudinal partitions.

On its side we find **ST. BERNARDINE ORATORY** with a beautiful Renaissance twofold portal with complicate floral motifs. In the lunette above it there is a bas-relief with the figure of St. Bernardine among Angels.

Now we are before the magnificent structure of the Basilica. We look first at the whole. On the lower part of the church we see the very beautiful portal leading to the LOWER CHURCH. On its left side rises the majestic structure of the Romanesque **Bell-tower**. It is quadrangular and has its walls divided vertically by prominent parastades and horizontally by cornices.

In the first and second large fillets are a mullioned window with two lights and another with three lights; in the third one, higher than the preceding ones, two mullioned windows, and another with three lights, almost create a portico. Higher than that we see three powerful round arcades on each side of the tower. This building dates back to 1239.

From the square a double, elegant and magnificent flight of steps leads to the Upper Basilica with a small bell-tower by its side.

# The Basilica of St. Francis

The story of the Basilica of St. Francis is very interesting. Unlike most of the religious buildings, it was planned and built in a relatively short time, though it was later beautified and enlarged. Fortunately its architectural plan was quite unitary as far as its general structure was concerned.

The Church has a quite originally articulated structure. At a glance its architectural structure is quite clear. The Basilica consists undoubtedly of only one magnificent building, but it is formed by churches placed one on the other and differently orientated, at least as far as their fronts are concerned, and, at the same time, they are so strictly connected one with the other as to give you the impression that you are before a complex whole.

It is sure that, since the beginning, the Church was conceived as double, specially because the steep ground with great differences in level did not allow to realize an unitary plan. It is also sure that the idea of building a basilica that would honour and keep the mortal remains of the Saint (temporarily kept in the Church of St. George) was practically contemporary with St. Francis' death or at most it rose a little later. We should also notice that this work was carried out in a very short time (if we except some decorative parts and later additions), mainly thanks to Brother Elia (who succeeded St. Francis as leader of the Order), to Pope Gregory IX and all the faithful that generously contributed to build the Basilica.

Most probably it was Brother Elia himself that planned the Church, not only because he patronized the project, but mainly because he indicated its architectural lines. It is very difficult to indicate all those who worked at this construction, though many names are mentioned in the chronicles of that time. It is sure that after Elia's death, but even previously, many architects took part in the construction of the Basilica, while after Elia's death it began to be beautified by many pictorial works. We know for sure also that in 1230 (St. Francis had died in 1226) the mortal remains of the "Poverello" were transferred into the crypt of the Lower Church. In 1253 the whole Basilica was practically finished, at least as far as its architectural structure was concerned, and in that very year it was consecrated by Pope Innocence IV.

As to the story of its paintings, we shall speak of it in details, while visiting the Basilica.

*Basilica of St. Francis*

*Portal of the Lower Church of St. Francis*

# The Lower Church

We are before the very elegant entrance portal of the Lower Church, a masterpiece of the Romanesque-Gothic art. It is preceded by only one round arch supported by two composite columns resting on quadrangular bases. Along the higher part is a short corona beautified by decorative festoons and two figures in bas-relief. Under the vault created by the arch, are two trilobate doors and a very fine rose-window. The whole is surrounded by a series of ogival arcades creating a soft-coloured surface.

This portal is beautified by fine polychromatic marbles and mosaics.

**The interior of the Church**: it is suggestive indeed, thanks to the wonderful combination of architecture and paintings, to the presence both of the Romanesque and Gothic styles. As a matter of fact, the bearing lines and the developments of its various parts are Gothic, while its general structure, based on the lowering of the arcades and vaults, is Romanesque. The whole is wrapped in a suggestive and religious atmosphere.

It is Latin-cross-shaped, with only one nave (with transept and apse), preceded by a wing reminding us of the ancient narthexes and animated by side chapels that were built later on. A series of big and short pillars support the lowered vaults, underlined and divided by finely decorated ribs.

Also the **transversal wing** that precedes the nave and is higher than the rest of the church, is divided into three parts. The vaults have been decorated by 17th century masters.

As we enter, on the left side is **St. Sebastian's Chapel**, where St. Francis' cowl, his shoes, the cloth by which he used to protect the wound on his chest, are exhibited in a niche.

On the opposite wall we can admire a fine **sepulchral monument** in Gothic style. After that we see a 15th century pulpit, whose original part dates back to the 14th century, adorned with fine polychromatic marble panels. It belonged to the Nepis family.

Then there is another sepulchre probably that of John of Brienne, emperor of Constantinople.

*Inside of the Lower Church - The Presbytery*
*The Four Veils: Poverty - Chastity - Obedience -*
*Triumph of St. Francis.*

At this point the transept, on its back, has a small chapel dedicated to St. Anthony. Near it there is the entrance to the **Cemetery**, situated in a middle-size cloister, but very suggestive for the wonderful combination of architecture and vegetation and its quiet atmosphere. Under a series of double arcades are some tombs.

We go back to the transversal wing of the church and just on the right side we find St. Catherine's Chapel built by Gattapone of Gubbio for Cardinal Albornoz in the 14th century. In it we can admire its beautiful glass windows (notice particularly that in the middle, attributed to the "Master of Figline") and the Crucifix of the altar, apart from the rich marble lining that characterizes this chapel. The frescoes by Andrea of Bologna (14th century) narrate the Martyrdom of the Saint.

We go back now to the centre of the church to begin the visit to its **nave**.

First of all we notice again the charm emanating from this part of the church with that play of light and shade and the vaults finely decorated and underlined by ribs. Some frescoes that unfortunately have been deteriorated and mutilated by the changes the church underwent during some widening works, and scarcely visible in the dark, represent scenes of the life of Christ (on the right wall) and of that of St. Francis (on the left wall). This wonderful pictorial complex, the oldest one decorating the Basilica, has been attributed to an unknown "Master of St. Francis". The artistic value of these paintings is undoubted. The figures are all placed on a compact background, but their simple, schematic, arcaic gestures express great incisiveness and strenght that cannot but draw the visitors' attention.

Our visit goes on starting from the first chapel to the left of the nave, **St. Martin's Chapel**. We are before a wonderful example of the refined art of Simone Martini who has decorated this chapel with a wonderful cycle of frescoes. The Chapel is characterized by flexible pictorial lines immerging all the figures in a mystical atmosphere. The frescoes represent some Saints and stories of St. Martin's life: St. Martin divides his cloak; he calls a child back to life; the Saint's funerals; his assumption in Heaven; he fights against his enemies with a cross in his hand; Jesus shows him the cloak he has donated; the Saint is meditating; he says Mass surrounded by angels; he is nominated knight. The lower part of the chapel is adorned with bi-coloured marbles forming some geometrical designs.

Going along the nave, we find the next **chapel**, that of **St. Peter of Alcantara**, small and quite bare. Along the walls of the nave is the **flight of steps** leading to St. Francis' Crypt we shall visit later. Then we see a marble pulpit in Cosmatesque style. Notice the fine representation of the "Coronation", unfortunately deteriorated.

Now we have reached the **Transept**.

First of all, we look at the **main altar** an elegant work in Gothic style.

Then we go along the **left wing** entirely decorated with a series of frescoes mostly by Pietro Lorenzetti and his assistants, among whom his brother Ambrogio. This artist, whose style is quite near to that of Giotto, expresses himself perhaps in a more arcaic language, but in some paintings he wonderfully combines figures and colours, as in some panels present in this church, for instance in the "Madonna" we shall see in a short while.

Among the various subjects concerning the stories of the Passion and the stories of St. Francis, stand out, for their pictorial incisiveness and harmonious composition, those of the "Crucifixion", "The Madonna with the Child and Saints", "The Deposition from the Cross". The latter draws our attention especially for the sense of tragedy it wonderfully expresses and for its animated figures.

*St. Martin's Chapel*
*(frescoed by Simone Martini)*
*St. Martin shares his cloak with a pauper*

*Opposite page:*
*St. Martin's Chapel*
*St. Francis*
*St. Clare*

Now we see all the panels in details.

Starting from left, in the first fillet along the vault, above the already mentioned "Crucifixion" and "Madonna with the Child", we find:
- The Scourging of Christ
- The Last Supper
- Jesus is arrested
- St. Francis receives the stigmata.

In the innermost fillet of the vault, starting again from the "Crucifixion", we find:
- Jesus climbs the Calvary
- Jesus enters Jerusalem
- The washing of the feet
- Judas hangs himself (the panel is small because there is a door).

On the back wall of the left wing of the transept we see:
- The Deposition of Christ from the Cross (a wonderful fresco full of pathos)(on the left)
- The Buring (on the right)
- The Resurrection of Christ (on the right)

The Chapel at the end of the left wing is dedicated to **St. John the Baptist** and keeps a fine painting by Pietro Lorenzetti representing the "Madonna with the Child, St. Francis and St. John", placed above the altar.

From here we reach the **Sacristes**, the first one with a fresco representing the "Madonna with the Child and the Saints Francis and Clare" executed probably by the "Master of Figline"; the other one is used mostly as treasure-room and reliquary, since it keeps many sacred and precious objects, among which St. Francis' hair-shirt.

Having visited the left wing of the Transept, we reach the **apse**, where we can admire the wonderful wooden choir in Gothic style, executed by various carvers and inlayers, the beautiful glass-windows and a 17th century fresco representing the "last Judgement".

Now let us have a look at the vault above the main altar. The complex of the frescoes that decorate it and have been attributed to Giotto for a long time, though they probably were executed by an unknown artist commonly called the "Master of the Sails", is divided into four sections representing the Allegories of the
- Apotheosis of St. Francis
- Chastity
- Poverty
- Obbedience

that, by a figurative language, explain the fundamental points of the Rule of the Franciscan Order.

We are now in the **right wing of the transept**. Also this part of the church is entirely and wonderfully frescoed. Giotto and some of his pupils worked at it. We look now at the paintings on the vault. Starting from left and following the outside fillet of the panels, we find:
- A little girl falling down from a window
- The Dispute in the Temple
- The Flight into Egypt
- The Nativity
- The Presentation of Jesus in the Temple
- The Madonna with the Child, Angels and St. Francis
- a wonderful fresco by Cimabue.

*"The crucifixion"*
*Pietro Lorenzetti*
*"Madonna of the Sunsets"*
*Pietro Lorenzetti*

*Opposite page:*
*"Madonna on Throne between the Angels and St. Francis" Cimabue 1280 about*
*"Nativity" - Giotto*
*"The Flight to Egypt" - Giotto*

In the innermost fillet of the vault, always from left, we see:
– St. Francis pointing at death
– Jesus leaves Jerusalem with his family
– The Slaughter of the Innocents
– The Visitation
– Epiphany
– Crucifixion.

We look now at the panels on the back wall.

On the upper part we find:
– Annunciation
– A child is extracted from some ruins (probably Dante and Giotto themselves are represented in this panel)
– The child comes back to life
– Figures of Saints (among which the beautiful portrait of St. Clare), placed along the lower fillet.

They are all by Simone Martini.

At the end of the right wing is **St. Nicholas' Chapel** built in the 13th century by Cardinal Orsini. The latter, unlike the symmetrical one in the left transept, has a fine cycle of frescoes representing episodes of the Saint's life and covering all the walls. These paintings, too, were executed by unknown artists, but they belong probably to Giotto's school.

From this chapel we reach that dedicated to **Mary Magdalen**, decorated by Giotto's pupils and by the Master himself. It was ordered by the bishop of Assisi, Tebaldo Pontano (his portrait is visible in one of the paintings). The frescoes represent mostly episodes of Mary Magdalen's life.

Now we go back to the nave and find the **Chapel of St. Anthony of Padua**, having gone beyond the Crypt we shall visit in a short while. It has been decorated by some of Giotto's pupils and by Sermei, an artist who was active in the 17th century.

Then comes St. Stephen's Chapel, with 16th century frescoes by Dono Doni, scenes of the Saint's life and other paintings by various artists.

Having visited the whole nave, we go to the entrance to the Crypt. The **Crypt** can be reached by a flight of steps leading into an underground room, now rearranged in order to keep St. Francis' body in a worthy manner. The corpse is kept in a stone urn protected by a glass, a structure in stonework and an iron grill. At the foot of the tomb is a simple altar for the celebration of the liturgies.

At the corners of the crypt are the urns containing the bones of some of the faithful companions of the Saint.

The whole crypt is very suggestive for its extreme simplicity, but mainly for the presence of the mortal remains of such a beloved Saint.

*Chapel of Magdalene - Noli me tangere - Giotto*

*The Tomb with sarcophagus containing the Saint's mortal remains*

*Opposite page: "St. Francis", by Cimabue (detail)*

# The Upper Church

We can reach it by a double flight of steps situated in the lower square or from the interior of the Church we have just visited, by a door situated in the right transept. In order to describe this Church better, we begin our visit going first to the upper square.

The beautiful building rises at the end of a wide green space that underlines the colours of the marbles and somehow helps to create a peaceful atmosphere.

Its **façade** forms an angle of 90° with that of the lower one and is divided into three sections by a cornice. Its lower part is adorned with an elegant, simple Gothic portal. The middle part has a very fine rose-window, while the upper part is cabin-shaped and has only one round window. Its style is substantially Gothic, and even though the bearing lines are very much semplified, the various elements of this art, so new for those times, mingle wonderfully in this building.

**The interior**: it is Gothic, with only one nave. The whole is quite luminous with those large glass-windows along all its perimeter. The space is here harmoniously divided and the frescoes are simply wonderful.

The nave has some composite pillars situated at regular intervals and including all the elements meant to divide the vault. A gallery runs along it at middle height. At the end of it are the transept and the polygonal apse. The temple of St. Francis seems to celebrate here the joy of life and the glory of God. The quiet and half-dark atmosphere of the lower church becomes much more luminous in the upper church and reaches moments of intense lyricism.

As we visit its interior, we shall consider two different factors, namely the cycles of homogeneous frescoes and their different ubication.

First of all we should see the great series of paintings along the walls of the nave. If we except four or five of them, they have been all attributed to Giotto. The frescoes of this cycle represent the most significant episodes of St. Francis' life.

In comparaison with all those who previously dealt with the same subject, Giotto looked at the Saint from a new view-point. He did not represent him as an ascetic, as a poor man spending most of his time in meditation, with his eyes turned to heaven, but as a true human being endowed with a strong will. In these panels, the figures and the space are set in opposite blocks. The sky itself is never represented as something airy, evanescent, but as something solid, as a volume set up against another volume. The various episodes are narrated synthetically but very clearly, because they are represented in their most significant moments. Giotto's narration becomes quite vivid and incisive, because all its parts are set up as they were architectural structures and the gestures of the various figures are incisive and dramatic. The whole acquires a new suggestive tension. In Giotto's hands, St. Francis' story developed by a means of various simple figures that are very vividly and finely outlined.

*Upper Church of St.
Francis - rose-window*

The theme of the cycle is drawn from the "Legenda major" of St. Bonaventure. Giotto chose all that he wanted out of such a rich material and represented all those episodes, that, according to him, were fit to outline St. Francis' figure and were more deeply felt by the artist. In this way the story of the "Poverello" becomes a human epic. Giotto refused all symbolic expressions and hyperboles, because all is reduced to a human dimension, where landscape plays an important role and, for the first time, the figures are slightly tridimensional.

Now we begin our visit starting form the nave and particularly from the right wall near the altar.

1 - In the square of Assisi, a cloak is donated to St. Francis in order to honour him (we see, in the panel, the Town Hall Square with its main buildings).

2 - St. Francis gives his cloak to a poor man (notice the landscape on the serene and harmonious background and the figures incisively outlined).

3 - St. Francis sees a palace full of arms meant for the Crusade.

4 - The Crucifix asks Francis to restore His house.

5 - St. Francis takes his clothes off before his father, taking the vow of poverty (notice the contrast between the calm but decise will of the Saint and the hardly checked anger of his father).

6 - Pope Innocence III dreams of Francis supporting the Church.

7 - The same Pope approves St. Francis' Rule.

8 - The vision of the cart of fire.

9 - The vision of the palace reserved in Heaven to St. Francis.

10 - St. Francis drives the devils out of the town of Arezzo (this painting is particularly interesting because the artist has tried to represent the town tridimensionally).

11 - St. Francis challenges the Muslims to an ordeal.

12 - St. Francis speaks with God, being in ecstasy.

13 - St. Francis makes the crib of Greccio (a very beautiful painting, at which also some assistants must have worked; the figures are represented as a whole and the perspective is quite good).

14 - St. Francis makes water spring (it is one of the most interesting and significant frescoes, because the representation is quite vivid, the narration is incisive and the figures and landscape mingle wonderfully together. Notice how the figure of St. Francis praving is underlined by its position within the pyramid-shaped mountain; notice also the dynamic figure of the thirsty man).

15 - St. Francis preaching to the birds (it is one of the most significant and touching frescoes of this cycle, a true poetical work. Notice the simple gesture of the Saint, the surprise of his companion, the birds that gather around St. Francis and the nature animated by a deep sense of peace.

16 - The death of the lord of Celano that had been foretold by St. Francis (a very dramatic scene).

17 - St. Francis preaching in the presence of Pope Honorius III (notice the intense expression of some faces).

18 - St. Francis appears to his friars at Arles.

19 - St. Francis receives the stigmata on Mt. La Verna (one of the most famous panels).

*Upper Church of St. Francis - inside*

20 - St. Francis' death (notice the expressive incisiveness of the lower part and the interesting perspective created by the bodies of the friars).

21 - St. Francis, after his death, appears to the bishop of Assisi.

22 - Noble Jerome becomes convinced of the reality of the stigmata.

23 - The transport of St. Francis corpse and the last greetings of St. Clare and her nuns (this panel, too, stands out for its expressiveness).

24 - The canonization of St. Francis (from his painting on we don't recognize Giotto's hand any more).

25 - The Saint appears to Gregory IX.

26 - St. Francis heals a wounded man.

27 - St. Francis resuscitates a dead man who confesses his sins.

28 - St. Francis sets Pietro di Alife free, since he had been unjustly charged with heresy.

We have gone through the whole nave. Now we have to see the upper part of wall, above Giotto's panels. Here are represented scenes from the Old and New Testaments attributed to Cimabue, to his school and partly also to Giotto himself (at the beginning of his career).

In order to complete the visit to the nave we have still to look at the vault of the church underlined and divided by the ribs that come up from the pillars, and the decoration of the whole, representing a starry sky. Figures of Saints and Doctors of the Church are represented in some of its sections.

We have now reached the **Transept** and the **Apse**. This part of the church is as interesting as the others we have seen till now, for its architectural structure (notice particularly the wonderful structure of the apse exalted by the magnificent glass-windows) and for its decorations, since here too the walls are entirely frescoed. The great artistic value of these paintings of this time due to the hand of another famous painter, Cimabue. His painting art can be considered as the conclusion of the Byzantine-like trends characterizing the art of his time. As he tried to be different, he was surely influenced by Giotto's new way of painting (according to tradition Giotto was one of Cimabue's pupils). Cimabue, however, succeeded in creating a great pathos in his works and obtained a better fusion and softness of colours, specially in the paintings characterizing the Upper Church of St. Francis.

*1) Young Francis is honoured by a humble man*

*4) St. Francis prays before the crucifix of St. Damian.*

2) *The Saint gives his cloak to a poor man on horseback.*

3) *The dream of the weapons.*

5) *St. Francis gives his clothes back to his father.*

6) *Innocenzo III dreams of the Saint upholding the falling Lateran.*

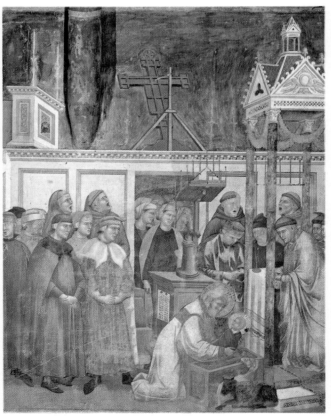

9) The vision of the celestial seats.

10) The expulsion of the demons from Arezzo.

14) The miracle of the spring- Opposite page

12) The ecstasy of St. Francis

13) St. Francis sets up the Christmas Crib at Greccio.

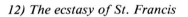

19) *St. Francis receives the stigmata on Mount Verna.*

22) *Checking the stigmata.*

20) *St. Francis death.*

15) *The preaching to the birds – Opposite page*

24) *The canonization of the Saint.*

**Left Transept**: we find in it: – a very fine "Crucifixion" by Cimabue, a work partly deteriorated, but still very expressive. Notice how the colours altered by time have created the negative image of the representation, if we except the gilding.
– some faded scenes from Revelation.

**Apse**: This cycle of frescoes has to be attributed to Cimabue and his assistants. It is quite deteriorated; it represents scenes of the Virgin's life.

A very beautiful choir follows the structure of the apse. It was made by 15th century carvers and inlayers. Notice particularly the decorations of the stalls representing famous friars and personages of that time. In the middle of the choir is the papal chair (a Cosmatesque work).

In the middle of the apse rises the main altar, a very fine and elegant Cosmatesque work dating back to the 13th century.

In the vault we admire some other frescoes by Cimabue, representing the Four Evangelists and the regions of the world conquered by Christianity.

**Right transept**: Most of the paintings covering the walls and vaults were executed by Cimabue and his assistants. Unfortunately they have deteriorated through the centuries and are not clearly visible in all their original beauty. They represent stories of the lives of St. Peter, St. Paul and Christ. A "Crucifixion" stands out in this wing, too.

Having examined all the frescoes, we should notice also the wonderful glass-windows situated along all the church up to the apse. Almost all date back to the 13th century; the designs are by various artists. They represent stories of the lives of St. Francis, St. Anthony, the Apostles, Angels, Prophets and the Madonna.

It may be very interesting to have a look at the church from the gallery situated half-way up along the nave.

*"Isaac repels Esau" (Giotto about 1292)*

*Opposite page:*
*"The four Doctors of the Latin Church"*
*(Giotto about 1292)*

*"Crucifixion" (Cimabue)*

# The complex of the Sacred Convent

From the Lower Church and the Upper Church, through doors situated along the right wing of the respective transepts, we can reach the architectural complex lying behind the Basilica. We are now practically in the magnificent building including the Sacred Convent.

From the outside, the **Sacred Convent** appeared to us as an imposing and huge system of buttresses. The high bastions on which the whole Basilica rests, seemed to us a true fortress watching over the whole town. As a matter of fact, this complex architectural system has been built in order to overcome the difficulties due to the quite steep ground in this area of Assisi. Consequently it was necessary to build solid and lasting foundations for the Basilica and all the buildings connected to it.

The huge and powerful complex of bastions was built mainly during the 14th century and continually enlarged and strenghtened. It was completed in the 15th century by order of Pope Sixtus V.

In the interior of the Sacred Convent are a series of halls used as meeting halls, dormitories, infirmary; it includes also a papal apartment.

Having come out of the Basilica of St. Francis, we have entered this building lying behind the church. First of all, once out of the two above mentioned small doors, let us look around us: we are in a large and airy terrace. From here we can admire the wonderful and dynamic structure of the apse of the Basilica. The construction looks majestic, superb.

In its middle part rises a polygonal building divided vertically by parastades and provided with three large windows. On its sides rise two cylindrical towers connecting the whole with the transepts.

From this same terrace our eyes sweep the large and airy **Cloister** that was built by Pope Sixtus IV in the 15th century. It consists of a double portico that still keeps a few deteriorated frescoes. In the middle of the cloister there is a well.

From this cloister we can reach the other parts of the Sacred Convent. The Chapter Hall, in a simple 13th century style, and the Refectory, where a large painting by Solimena is kept, are worth visiting. Then we can reach the magnificent **Portico** facing the valley below and presenting a wonderful landscape. It rests on the buttresses below with its powerful system of arcades.

Now we go to the halls that keep the

# Treasure

This is a true Museum that keeps paintings and precious objects donated by the pilgrims – often famous personages – who have come here to visit and honour the Saint of Assisi.

Though it was often deprived of many of its precious objects, the Treasure is still quite rich and interesting.

The collection is kept in two halls and, if we except the paintings, all the objects are kept in special show-cases.

*Sistus IV's Cloister and apse*

*Opposite page:*
*The colonnade (XIII C.), in the*
*background the plains of Umbria crossed*
*by the Tescio river.*

# The Town Hall Square

We are now in the political and administrative heart of Assisi and practically in the heart of the ancient Roman Municipium of Asisium, since the temple of Minerva, rising in this square, was set in the ancient Roman Forum still visible in the area below the same square.

This area, however, even after such a long time, is still the historical centre of the town, even if at present the religious centre is the area around the Basilica of St. Francis.

The square is rectangular and quite oblong. The various streets of the town, lying at different levels because of the terraced ground, all meet in it.

In the middle is a beautiful and simple polygonal fountain, preceded by flights of steps on one side and close to the street on the other, because of the asymmetric ground.

Above the basin is a polygonal marble bowl surmounted by a composite sculpture. In the basin, the water comes out of the mouths of three lions.

Since we have reached the square from the side of the streets coming from the Basilica of St. Francis, we shall begin our visit from this point.

Just where Portica Street meets the square we can see the 14th century **PULPIT**. In the interior is a fresco by Simone Martini, representing the "Madonna among Angels". Though it has deteriorated, we can still admire the deep lyricism and sweetness of the pictorial lines of this great artist.

On the left side of the square we find the **PEOPLE'S CAPTAIN'S PALACE**, a beautiful 13th century building with large arcades in its lower part and two orders of windows in the upper part. It has also an embattled corona. When Assisi was a Free Town, this Palace was the seat of the People's Captain. In the 20th century it was the Mayor's residence. At present it houses the Society of Franciscan Studies.

Near the Palace rises the **TOWER**, with imposing structures in Romanesque style. It has Ghibelline battlements, while those of the palace are Guelph. It was built in the 13th century, but it was completed at the beginning of the following century. One gets inside it by a very fine portal.

Then comes the often mentioned **TEMPLE OF MINERVA**, a wonderful example of Roman imperial architecture. Thanks to its ancient beauty and the solemn harmony of its lines, it strikes the visitors, considering also the contrast between it and the surrounding environment. But, most of all, it wonderfully bears witness to the splendour of the Roman Assisi.

From it we reach the ancient cell that, in the middle of the 16th century, was transformed into the **Church of St. Mary above Minerva**, so called in order to remind us of the pagan temple on which it was built.

We go around the square looking at various buildings, till we reach the opposite side, just in front of the People's Captain's Palace. Here we find the **PRIOR'S PALACE** dating back to the 14th century. It consists of various buildings of different size, but all in the same style. A part of it still shows the Guelph battlement, while the others are simply covered with ordinary roofs. Along its front are various lowered arcades. The decoration of the large arch leading to the Pinta vault is very interesting. In the upper part are various windows all characterized by the same austere simplicity.

*The town hall square*
*Crypt of San Nicolò now Roman Museum*

*Opposite page:*
*Etruscan cinerary urn*

*The Municipality square with Minerva's Temple, the Civic Tower and the Palace of the Captain of the People.*

*The Corporation of Notaries coat of arms on the door of the Tower.*

From the above mentioned large arch we can admire the back of the Prior's Palace that, thanks to its structures, looks like a fortified house. We are now in the New Church Square, where the **NEW CHURCH** rises. Its interesting interior is in Renaissance style, while its exterior is in Baroque style. According to tradition, this church keeps the prison in which St. Francis was closed by order of his father who was trying to bring him back to his old way of living.

We go back to the square and visit the **PICTURE-GALLERY** situated, together with the municpal offices, in the Prior's Palace.

The collection of paintings here kept is riche and quite interesting. There are sculptures coming from various parts of Italy. In the Picture-Gallery, the Umbrian painting is largely represented. Its various schools and numerous artists have made Assisi and its environs even more beautiful. Simone Martini, Matteo di Gualdo, Dono Doni, Giorgetti, Sermei are perhaps the most known names, but many other artists worked here. Thanks to them, it is possible to have a quite ample picture of the stylistic trends present in the town and in Umbria, that have beautified churches and palaces for a long time.

**THE ORATORY OF THE INFANT ST. FRANCIS**. This oratory was built towards the end of the 13th century on the site where, according to tradition, St. Francis was born. As a matter of fact, Pietro Bernardone and his wife Pica, St. Francis' parents, lived in the upper part of the building. According to another tradition, on the ground floor there was a stable, and it was there that Pica, heavenly inspired,, went to give birth to her son. The people's devotion has identified the birth of the "Poverello" with that of Christ.

*New Church*
*San Francesco Piccolino - the stable where the Saint was supposedly born*

*Opposite page:*
*The three doors to Saint Francis' father's house*

*The prison where Francis was locked by his father*

*St. Francis father's house - the place indicated as a store*

FRANCISCVS · INCLV
SVS · FVIT · A · PATRE

# The Cathedral
## (Church of St. Ruphinus)

Our attention is immediately drawn by the beautiful façade that with its harmonious and well divided surfaces, constitutes one of the finest example of the Romanesque style, though it has been influenced by local trends. Near it the beautiful bell-tower rises high and imposing.

The Cathedral was once a very small church meant to keep the mortal remains of St. Ruphinus, bishop of the town (III century). It was later enlarged and modified. Its present look is that due to Giovanni of Gubbio (in the 12th century), as indicated by a marble-stone situated inside the church. The works, however, went on even after the middle of the 13th century.

### The exterior:

The big and austere bell-tower consists of an older part (till the clock) and another part contemporary with the church, animated by small pensile arches and windows. Il rests on a Roman cistern visible from the interior of the church.

### The façade:

In its lower section it has the surfaces divided into large and well marked panels animating the architecture with a delicate play of light and shade. A large portal with a round arch opens in the middle of it (two smaller ones are on its sides). Their decorations are quite rich and refined and consist of classical motifs. In the lunette of the middle portal are represented Christ between the Sun and the Moon, the Madonna and St. Ruphinus. Some rampant animals are represented in the side ones. Some beautiful marble lions lie at the base of the entrance door.

Above this first section runs a low but elegant gallery. A little higher are three fine rose-windows, of which the middle one is larger and surrounded by sculptures with the symbols of the Evangelists and some animals.

The upper part of the façade, separated from that below by a series of small pensile arches, is different as far as style and proportions are concerned. As a matter of fact, it was the last part to be built and was not even completed. Probably a painting or a mosaic had to be set in the large ogival arcade animating this section.

### The interior

It has a nave and two aisles. It was transformed in the 16th century by the architect Galeazzo Alessi, who strenghtened also its structures. (The same artist built the church of St. Mary of the Angels). Though this work was necessary, the whole church was damaged from a stylistic view-point. Many decorations, too, have been added in the following centuries. Consequently we mention here only those works that seem to us more worthy of your attention:

– the baptismal font (at the beginning of the right aisle), consisting of a granitic block enclosed and protected by an iron grill. It was here that St. Francis and St. Clare were baptized.

*Cathedral*

*Opposite page:*
*The Church of St. Ruphinus - Inside*
*Christening bath*
*Crypt*
*Sarcophagus of III c. showing the myth of*
*Diana and Endymion*

– "Crucifixion" and "Deposition" by Dono Doni (situated above the altars on the sides of the main altar).

– the carved and inlaid Choir, a precious work dating back to the 16th century.

– "Pietà" (in the Chapel of Our Lady of Tears), an original and expressive work of painted terracotta due to German artists.

– two sculptures by Dupré (father and son), dating back to the 19th century.

From the right side of the church we can reach the **Capitular Museum** that keeps some of the remaining architectural structures of the preceding constructions, besides some paintings of historical and artistic value. A polyptych by Alunno, representing the "Madonna among Saints" stands out of the others. In the Museum are also paintings coming from other religious buildings, ornaments and richly and patiently decorated codices.

Still in the interior of the church, by a door situated along the left aisle, we can reach the Roman **Cistern**, on which the bell-tower of the Cathedral has been built.

In order to complete our visit to the church, we go down into the **Crypt** (the sacristan will accompany you there). It was built a little after the year 1000. The whole is quite suggestive, specially thanks to its peculiar structure. Notice the pillars, with those peculiar capitals, forming the small portico, and, in the interior, the remains of frescoes and the Roman sarcophagus with mythical representations. St. Ruphinus was buried in this place.

# The Church of St. Clare

It was built in the middle of the 13th century. It is dedicated to the other great daughter of Assisi, the companion of St. Francis and foundress of the Order of the Poor Clares.

In spite of the different structure of its side parts, this Church reminds us of the outside and inside structure of the Upper Church of St. Francis. Its façade is characterized by alternating white and pink stones that create large longitudinal fillets. In its lower part is a portal with a round arch, but in Gothic style, underlined by a corona resting on two lions. A very fine rose-window dominates it.

On the left side of the church a magnificent arch leans against the construction in order to support the whole structure. Other two arches are along the same side creating an imposing complex, especially for the suggestive play of light and shade created by the arches.

On the other side corresponding to the façade there is a parallelepipedal body that, in the interior of the church, creates a chapel.

The **interior** is in Gothic style and, as the Upper Church of St. Francis, has one nave divided into four spans. But the impression it makes on the visitors is quite different, not only because there are no frescoes, but mainly because it is not as luminous as its model.

The **nave** is now bare.

Near the fourth span, on the right side, there is a chapel that was once the ancient church of **St. George**, where the body of St. Francis was kept before it was transferred in the Basilica of St. Francis. It is Gothic style and divided into two chapels, that of the Sacrament and that of the Crucifix. In both of them we can admire an interesting series of frescoes executed by different schools, and in particular there is the **Crucifix** (from which it derives its name) that, according to tradition. in the ruined church of St. Damian, ordered Francis to rebuild His house.

Here are kept also some relics, such as the cowls of St. Francis and St. Clare, the hair St. Clare cut by herself, when, still a young girl, she took the vow of poverty, and a breviary.

Having gone back to the nave, we may go down into the **crypt**, where the body of St. Clare is kept in a recently built Gothic-like shrine.

Again near the fourth span, we can reach St. Agnes Chapel.

Let us reach now the apse and the transept.

**The left transept**: some paintings representing stories of the Old Testament and dating back to the 13th and 14th centuries; a very fine "Crib".

**In the Presbytery**: in the middle is a beautiful altar surrounded by an elegant marble colonnade. On the vault, divided into four sections, are represented the "Madonna" and some Saints among Angels. In the area of the apse we can admire a fine "Crucifix" dating back to the 13th century and attributed to an unknown Master of St. Clare's. The painting has also some smaller panels with various images of the Madonna, St. Francis and St. Clare.

**Right Transept**: On the back wall we find some "Stories of the New Testament". Besides that, another painting represents St. Clare and some stories of her life. Its author is unknown. Some critics have attributed it to the Master of St. Clare's, but others think that it might be one of Cimabue's works. The stories surround the figure of St. Clare and start from the panel below, on the left:

(1) The bishop gives an olive-branch to St. Clare.
(2) St. Clare leaves her father's house in order to follow St. Francis' example.
(3) St. Clare wears very simple clothes and takes the vow of poverty.
(4) Her father tries to bring her home again.
(5) Her sister Agnes follows Clare's example and opposed her father who is trying to bring her back to her old way of living.
(6) St. Clare blesses some loaves of bread.
(7) The Madonna appears to dying St. Clare.
(8) St. Clare's funeral.

*Church of St. Clare*

*Opposite page:*
*The Manger crib: fresco of the Umbrian - Sienese school in the left transept*
*The Crucifix which spoke to St. Francis in 1206 in the small church of San Damiano (XII c.)*
*St. Clare and eight stories of her life - painting attributed to Cimabue: in right transept*

**THE CHURCH OF ST. MARY MAJOR**. It has kept the simple Romanesque structures dating back to the 12th century. It took the place of a preceding Christian building that had been built on the site of a pagan temple, as it is shown by some finds and inscriptions from which we deduce that it was probably dedicated to Apollo.

**THE CHURCH OF ST. PETER**. It is another wonderful example of the Romanesque-Gothic architecture of Assisi.

The church is very old. It was built by the Benedictine Order probably in the 10th century or, more probably, at the beginning of the 11th century. It was, however, modified and partly rebuilt in the 13th century and consacrated after the middle of the same century.

**THE CHURCH OF ST. JAMES DE MURO RUPTO** (of the broken wall), so called after a nearby tower in ruins.

**THE CHURCH OF ST. STEPHEN** a very simple building dating back to the 12th century, but completed only in the 13th century. Its walls are made of rough stones, as almost all the houses of Assisi.

**THE CHURCH OF ST. PAUL** whose construction ended in the 13th century. It has a Romanesque look and a fresco by Dono Doni adorning its bare façade. The interior, with one nave, is very peaceful; there is a 15th century fresco by Matteo di Gualdo.

**THE CHURCH OF THE CAPUCHINS** set into a medieval house with its typical door of the dead. (This is a characteristic element of many ancient towns. It was a small door situated near a larger one. According to tradition, it was so called because the corpses were let out of the house through it. Most probably, however, it was the real entrance door, situated on a level higher than that of the street for safety's sake.

**THE PILGRIMS ORATORY**. It was once an hospital. The building has 15th century structures, but it is even older. The interior is very interesting, because it is entirely decorated by frescoes of which some are attributed to Matteo di Gualdo and Mezzastris; the "Madonna among Angels and Saints" is particularly beautiful.

**THE PORTICO OF MOUNT FRUMENTARIO**. In the 13th century it was an hospital for poor people. It became later the seat of the Bank of the Barberini family.

This construction consists of seven arcades delimited by simple columns resting on a base (except one used as an entrance portal).

Immediately after the portico, we find the **OLIVIERA FOUNTAIN** with an elegant and harmonious 16th century structure. Its consists of a basin and an abutment divided into panels delimited by projecting curvilinear structures.

**THE MARCELLA FOUNTAIN**, a finely decorated and divided rectangular basin. It dates back to the 16th centuy. On the opposite side we can admire the beautiful and suggestive view of the plain below Assisi.

**THE ORATORY OF ST. LEONARD** or of **ST. FRANCESCUCCIO** (little Francis). Its 14th century façade with a very simple Gothic portico is adorned with a fine fresco situated in a sort of niche below the penthouse. In the interior, too, are some interesting paintings, among which a very fine one representing the "Crucifixion", situated on the back of the altar. The Oratory is now the seat of a Fraternity.

**ROCCA MAGGIORE**. This fortress is very beautiful for its position dominating wide landscapes, and for the complex structure of its parts. It was the stronghold of the town of Assisi and already existing in the 12th century. It was later strengthened and enlarged because of its great strategic importance.

It is trapezoidal and animated by towers. In the middle there is the main tower including a quadrangular body. From it start the walls surrounding the town and a passage connected with a polygonal tower built by Pope Pius II in the 15th century.

Before leaving the Rock, let us have another look at the imposing and harmonious structure of this fortress that is certainly one of the most interesting and beautiful fortresses of the Middle Ages. Our eyes sweep the town of Assisi, the quiet plain below and the slopes of Mt. Subasio. We enjoy again, for a little while, the view of this corner of Umbria so sweet for its landscape, so suggestive for the wonderful combination of natural and artistic elements, so significant for its historical and religious memories.

*Church of St. Mary Major*

*Opposite page:*
*Church of St. Peter*
*Church of St. Stephen*
*The Rocca Maggiore*

# The hermitage of the Prisons

We can reach it going out of Assisi through Matteotti Square and the Capuchins Gate. At present it can be easily reached by car, thanks to a wide junction road. Once it was not so, especially in the times of St. Francis, when only a narrow path lead from the town to the retreat of his companions.

As a matter of fact, the hermitage is situated on the slopes of Mt. Subasio. This place was chosen by St. Francis and his followers, since it was fit for a life of contemplation and meditation.

The church and the adjoining convent, at the end of a short path, resting on the steep ground and rock, once did not exist. For St. Francis and his companions this place of recollection and prayer was only a cave near a little chapel and the ground was their bed, as we can still clearly see.

Since the Franciscan Friars went on frequenting this place for a long time, little by little rose the first buildings that brought to the construction of the cells of the convent, the refectory and the little church. The whole was carried out at the beginning of the 15th century specially under the direction of St. Bernardine of Siena.

The visit to the Hermitage of the Prisons (so called after the image of the "Madonna of the Prisons", a painting kept in the old chapel) is very suggestive not only for the religious and mystical atmosphere characterizing all the places where the Saint lived and worked, but also for the deep silence reigning everywhere, for the extreme semplicity characterizing the whole environment, the cells, the bare refectory, all bearing witness to the true humility of the Saint and his companions.

Going beyond a wooden door, we reach first a small quiet courtyard (with a well in the middle) opening on to a precipice. The view we enjoy from here makes our sense of solitude grow and we realize how much this construction has been daring and how beautiful these places are. Places loved by St. Francis, all very similar, since they are far from the town, solitary among the mountains, where nature is incontaminated and the creation shows all its beauty and magnificence.

In the interior we can visit the refectory. It is a very simple and quiet room close to the rocky walls of the mountain. The cells of the convent are very simple and poor. Then there are the little church, the primitive chapel with the image of the "Madonna of the Prisons", the grottoes where St. Francis used to pray and sleep. As we can see, his bed was simply the bare stone.

Now we may take a walk to the nearby wood, a place of prayer and meditation for so many Franciscan Friars, as it is shown by the numerous caves spread all over this place, where they loved to give themselves to a solitary contemplation.

*Hermitage of the prisons*
*The small Cloister*

*Opposite page:*
*An age-old holm-oak which reminds of the*
*Saints conversations with the birds*
*The Chapel of the Virgin*
*St. Francis' cave*

# St. Damian's

This is one of the most worth visiting places in Assisi, since it is strictly connected with its history and with that of St. Francis. Besides that, the church keeps precious artistic testimonies of the past.

We can reach it from the New Gate, after a short walk.

It is the church which St. Francis and his companions restored after he heard the words of the Crucifix inviting him to restore His house. The young man was then among the ruins of this solitary building when, according to the tradition, he heard the voice of Christ coming from the painting situated above the altar (this Crucifix is now in the church of St. Clare). Consequently he did his best to restore the temple of the Lord to its former beauty. Here came also St. Clare who lived in this place with her sisters for a long time.

Most probably it was here that St. Francis composed that beautiful prayer called the Canticle of the Creatures.

The church and the surrounding environment constitute an oasis of peace and religious silence, which is the most common feature of the churches of Assisi and of the town itself.

Now let us have a good look at St. Damian's.

The church has a very simple **façade** preceded by a low portico. A simple rose-window is above the central arch, but it is decentralized in respect to the whole building. On the right side of the arcades rises a chapel, where we can see a fresco representing the "Madonna among St. Francis, St. Clare and other Saints" (15th century).

Under the portico, always on the right side, is another small chapel, called St. Jerome's Chapel, decorated with 15th century frescoes.

The **interior**, immersed in a faint light, is very simple. It has one nave ending with a quite long choir. The whole is very suggestive. It looks more like a cave than like a religious building. St. Francis must have felt himself at ease in such a place, being in close contact with nature. Besides that, the temple of the Lord was free from any decoration and earthly vanity.

**Right wall**: notice, first of all, the little window and the fresco divided into three sections all representing an episode of St. Francis life connected with St. Damian's: 1) He is invited by the Crucifix to restore His house. 2) St. Francis throws the money, obtained from the sale of his father's fabrics and refused by the priest-guardian of the church, out of the window (that we see at the beginning of the nave). 3) Francis' father reproaches him for having wasted that money. These paintings date back to the 14th century.

Then we find the Crucifix's Chapel, where is kept an interesting and original wooden Crucifix, one of the works of Innocenzo of Palermo (17th century). The peculiar feature of this Crucifix is that it takes various expressions depending on the various visual angles (notice the expressions of suffering, delirium, death).

**Apse**: above the main altar is a copy of the painting representing the "Crucifixion" that, according to tradition, spoke to St. Francis.

In the upper part is another fresco, quite deteriorated and dating back probably to the 14th century.

A very simple wooden choir (16th century) is situated along the apse. Notice the inscription along the stalls that, translated into English, runs so: «It is the vow, not the voice, the love, not the noise, the heart, not the string that reaches the Lord's hear».

Now we enter a **Vestibule**, where is a rustic wooden choir, in which St. Clare and her sisters gathered. Notice the very simple kneeling-stool and lectern.

Through the vestibule we go up to a small and beautiful **garden**. It is really a small terrace, a very quiet and simple open space. Here our eyes sweep a wide stretch of the surrounding countryside. A slab of marble on the wall reminds us that probably it was here that St. Francis composed his Canticle of the Creatures. St. Clare used to retire often into his place.

Then we reach St. Clare's **Oratory**. It is a simple hall, partly frescoed, with an apse. Here are kept various relics of the Saint and the Ostensory that, according to an oral tradition, she showed to the Saracens in order to drive them out of the town.

Then we enter the dormitory: it was here that St. Clare died in 1253.

We go on and reach the **cloister**, a very pleasant, silent and quiet place, adorned with green plants and vases that during Spring and Summer contain variously coloured flowers. Its style is simple, rustic, with round arcades resting on a low wall. On one side we can admire the simple bell-tower and the back of the church, while in the middle is a well-parapet.

We enter now St. Clare's Refectory. This very simple hall is quite suggestive. There is a religious and mystical atmosphere created by those seats and walls, on which time has left indelible marks and where is still alive the memory of the poor, obedient monastic life that has always characterized the Order of the Poor Clares. All in this refectory has remained as it was in the times of St. Clare and all things here tell us of that age, the old tables, the blackened surfaces. There are also some frescoes by Dono Doni and a "Crucifixion„ all works that, though deteriorated, also speak the mystical language of this place.

We may visit also the **Infirmary** situated on the upper floor.

*Church of San Damiano*

*Opposite page:*
*Inside*
*St. Clare's refectory*
*The Cloister*
*The slope of cypresses*

# Feasts and traditions of Assisi

CALENDIMAGGIO or May-Day is so called because "calendae" meant the first day of a month, according to the Roman calendar. This is, therefore, a feast of profane origin, though, even on this occasion, people try to commemorate also Francis and his thoughtless youth. It takes place between the last day of April and the first day of May. It is an outburst of joy and freshness, of songs and sounds, of traditional costumes and flowers. It is the celebration and exaltation of Spring that expresses itself in the people and things with the joy of life. This festival is quite felt by the people of Assisi that take part in it wearing their traditional costumes. Its aim is the conquest of the "palio" (a symbolic finely decorated cloth), disputed by the "upper part" and the "lower part", the two quarters into which the town is divided. The judges give the "palio" to the part that has distinguished itself for its costumes, songs, flagwaving, and in the cross-bow archers' competitions.

Among the religious feasts that of the PARDON OF ASSISI is quite important. It commemorates the indulgence obtained by St. Francis on the occasion of the official approval of his Rule from Pope Honorius III, for all those who would go to the Porziuncola asking God to forgive their sins. This feast takes place from July 31 to August 2, drawing here crowds of pilgrims coming from all parts of the world.

Other religious feasts take place to commemorate St. Francis' death (October 4) and that of St. Clare (August 12). Other feasts are connected with more important feasts, such as the Holy Week, Ascension Day, Pentecost, Corpus Domini. Particularly interesting and suggestive are those connected with the Holy Week, including processions along the streets of the town, with hooded friars bearing crosses and the symbols of Christ's Passion, other monks and people bearing torches. It takes place also the "Deposition from the Cross and the descent of the Madonna near to her Son's Body», after the style of some ancient religious plays.

Worth mentioning are also the processions and the rites celebrated on various days of the month (on Fridays and Sundays) and taking place after sunset, when the Franciscan Friars file off in the Basilica of St. Francis and in the square before it in order to commemorate the Saint and some episodes of his life.

Though such ceremonies and feasts are mainly religious, they are almost all characterized also by other features, such as historical and cultural commemorations that give a special charm to them, accompanied as they are by the people that parade wearing their colourful, costumes, and by traditional rites.

# The Church of St. Mary of the Angels

The visit to the church of St. Mary of the Angels completes that to Assisi, since, as many other places and churches characterizing this area, it is strictly connected with the life and activity of St. Francis. It is a place of worship where, perhaps more than elsewhere, is alive the memory of that exceptional man who wanted to die in the simple chapel that had seen the beginning of his spiritual ministry. These very significant facts and the Pardon's indulgence connected with the Porziuncola, have always drawn to St. Mary of the Angels crowds of pilgrims.

The church rises in the plain, at the foot of Assisi. We have already seen it rising with its imposing architectural structure, while going up to the town, and we have admired it from the town, recognizing its slender dome and the glittering golden statue of the Madonna.

We can reach it leaving Assisi from St. Peter's Gate. We go beyond the regional Seminary and **Gualdi House**, once used as hospital for the lepers. Then we reach the village of St. Mary of the Angels, densely populated and modern, risen around the Basilica.

Just below the dome, where the wings of the transept meet the nave and the two aisles, is the

## THE PORZIUNCOLA

As we have said, the church of St. Mary of the Angels was built in order to preserve this place, in which St. Francis stayed for a long time and founded his religious Order. Its story is quite old and it is worth telling again.

This very simple and bare chapel was built probably in the 4th century A.D., perhaps in order to keep a relic of Our Lady's sepulchre. It might derive its name either from "a portion of stone" or from "a portion of ground", since it was built in a very small piece of ground. It is certain that it belonged to the Benedictine Order till St. Francis chose this place as his own residence, considering its poverty and solitude.

With the Porziuncola is connected also the Pardon's Indulgence St. Francis obtained when the Pope approved his Ruel officially. The feast of the Pardon is celebrated at the beginning of August.

In this solitary and out-of-hand place gathered the Franciscan Friars, who used to come here to discuss and improve the principles of their Rule, as St. Francis himself had established to do. As a matter of fact, many very poor cabins rose in the little wood that once was in this area. In 1221 the Friar's Chapter, namely the meeting of the Franciscans coming from all parts of Europe, was attended by 5000 friars and was called the Chapter of the Mats.

It was in this Porziuncola that Francis wanted to be transferred when he felt he was leaving this life, because he trought it was here he had begun his spiritual activity.

St. Clare's life, too, is connected with these places, because she came here and took the vows of poverty, chastity and obedience, being enthusiast for Francis' peaching, when she decided to consacrate herself completely to Christ's love.

Now let us describe the Porziuncola. Its front is now adorned with a Gothic-like façade surmounted by a tabernacle. Here is a worth admiring fresco, dating back to the 19th century and covering preceding frescoes that represented the same subject.

*The Cloister*

**Interior**: here the extreme poverty and humility of the environment is even more evident. Here the memories of St. Francis crowd and tell again of the activity of this man who ended his life in an examplary way, as he had lived. At present this interior, still so suggestive, is enlightened by pensile lamps and a 14th century painting placed along the ogival back wall: it represents the "Annunciation" surrounded by stories of the Saint's life, by Ilario of Viterbo.

Also on the sides and back of the Porziuncola there are remains of frescoes and a terra-cotta representing St. Francis. There is also the tomb of a Friar, namely Blessed Pietro of Catania.

Let us reach now the back of the Porziuncola. On the right side there is the **Chapel of the Passing away**, where St. Francis died on the bare ground, as poor as he had lived.

It was originally a place meant to house sick people. Later one, in order to honour the "Poverello" of Assisi, it was transformed into a chapel.

On the outside, it has now a 19th century fresco representing the Saint's death.

In the interior are other frescoes and a beautiful statue of enamelled terra-cotta, by Andrea della Robbia, representing the Saint.

We may now visit the new crypt that has been recently built, the wonderful terracotta polyptych by Andrea della Robbia, once set in altar of the left wing of the transept. It represents stories of Our Lady and St. Francis, on a glowing blue background.

We reach now the Sacresty (from the right wing) keeping very elaborate 17th century furniture, then a passage where is a statue of St. Francis, where the turtle-doves love to rest. After a portico, in a pleasant open space, is another statue of the Saint with a sheep, bearing witness to the love the "Poverello" of Assisi always showed to all the creatures of nature.

Then we reach the Rosery keeping plants of roses without thorns. According to a legend, the roses deprived themselves of thorns in order not to harm St. Francis, when he threw himself among them, without clothes, to avoid temptations and mortify his body.

We are now in the little **Chapel of the Roses**, consisting of three rooms frescoed by Tiberio of Assisi with episodes of St. Francis' life (quite interesting), among which the episode of the rosery and other illustrating the Rule. These rooms were built at different times by St. Bonaventure and St. Bernardine. Here is also St. Francis grotto, where he used to sleep.

We may go on visiting the **old Convent** that, begun in St. Francis' times, was successively enlarged. In its cloister are many archaeological finds, a well (where according to a sacred tradition, water sprang by order of St. Francis) ad a Romanesque transenna.

In a little chapel of the Convent is a beautiful majolica picture representing "St. Francis weeping" (hence the name of **Chapel of the Weeping**), similar to that existing in Greccio, another very important Franciscan centre, where he had the idea of a living Crib.

*Porziuncola Chapel*
*Inside*
*Chapel of the Passing*

*Opposite page:*
*Porziuncola Chapel*

Lastly we visit the **MUSEUM** of the Basilica keeping, in the first section, sacred furniture, reliquaries and precious objects. In the second section are some paintings by Mezzastris, Alunno, Sano di Pietro and those particularly beautiful and significant by Giunta Pisano ("Crucifixion"), by St. Francis' Master ("St. Francis among Angels") and perhaps by Cimabue ("Crucifix").

In the Museum are also various halls keeping mainly ethnographic testimonies. Other halls keep furniture and instruments dating back to various ages, besides the Library (with fine codices and interesting prints) and the Pharmacy with a fine collection of vases.

We may conclude our visit to the Church of St. Mary of the Angels by reaching the cloister of the present Convent facing the square before the church.

*St. Francis and the doves*
*The rose-garden*
*St. Francis' cave*

*Opposite page:*
*Museum of the Basilica*
*"Crucifix" by Giunta Pisano*
*St. Francis between two Angels*
*Maestro di San Francesco*
*Chapel of Tears*

# Gubbio

Gubbio is situated in northern Umbria, on the edge of a well-defined plateau, enclosed between the folds of the Appennines. Standing at an altitude of approximately 500 metres, it lies on the slopes of Monte Ingino, Monte Calvo (or Foce) and Monte San Girolamo. The town is traversed by two small mountain rivers, the Camignano and Cavarello, which further down valley debouch into the river Saonda and successively into the Chiascio.

The town, which has a population of some 15,000 today, is one of the most suggestive and unique not only in Umbria, but in Italy as a whole, for its unmistakeable and mercifully unaltered medieval appearance, its splendid monuments, its countless historical and artistic testimonies, its ancient and traditional handicrafts, and its celebrated "Corsa dei Ceri" whose fame has reached every corner of the world.

Commonly and justly called Italy's "most beautiful medieval town", Gubbio thus preserves intact its ancient townscape, buildings, streets and works of art from that far-off period. Divided into the quarters of San Martino, San Giuliano, Sant'Andrea and San Pietro, it is surrounded almost entirely by the ancient walls built (in the 12th century) by the bishop St. Ubaldus in defence of the town, as part of his plan to rebuild it on the slopes of Monte Ingino instead of down on the plain below, where it had previously been sited and where it had suffered a series of destruction and fires. This circuit of walls is fortified by numerous towers, and pierced by various gates: Metauro, Castello, Degli Ortacci, Vittoria, Romana and Sant'Ubaldo.

Gubbio's road system essentially consists of five roughly parallel streets (the Corso Garibaldi, Via Savelli, Via dei Consoli, Via XX Settembre, Via Mazzini and Via Reposati) which probably reproduce the street pattern, of Roman Iguvium. These main longitudinal axes are intersected by a network of little streets, alleys and stairways, characteristically steep and narrow, and often picturesque in their constantly varying alternation of different prospects.

The houses of Gubbio mainly date to the Middle Ages and thus generally preserve the style of that period. They are built out of the grey stone quarried from the mountains that surround Gubbio or in a mixture of stone and brick.

Recurrent features of the architecture of these houses include the ogival arch and the so-called "door of the dead". This latter is a smaller, raised door (above street level), also with a pointed arch, and flanking a larger door situated on the ground floor (this was generally the entrance to the shop).

According to tradition, this raised door was the exit once reserved for the dead (hence its name). More probably, however, it was the actual entrance to the house, which was once equipped with a wooden stairway; this was pulled up into the inside at night. But it seems that it was on this stairway that the body of the deceased was exposed to the piety and prayers of kinsmen and friends: a fact that concurred in some measure to give the door its name.

*Porta Romana*
*Porta Sant'Ubaldo*
*Porta Metauro*
*Porta Vittoria*

# Historical and artistic background

The area around Gubbio was inhabited since pre-historic times, as is demonstrated by a number of unequivocal finds, made on Monte Calvo and also by the cyclopean walls (later in date) visible in the environs of the hermitage of Sant'Ambrogio.

The town itself, though was founded under the Umbri (the ancient, pre-Roman people of Umbria). It then had the name of Ikuvium, and soon rose into a flourishing and powerful centre, as is testified by the "Eugubine Tablets", a series of bronze inscriptions which represent the most important historical and religious document of this ancient Italic civilization (the "Eugubine Tablets" will be discussed more specifically below during our description of the Museum in the Palazzo dei Consoli in which they are displayed).

From the 3rd century B.C. onwards, after it had entered into an alliance with Rome, the Umbrian town progressively fell under the influence, and then under the rule, of Rome, until being eventually included in the Clustumina Tribe. During this period it had the name of Iguvium; was embellished with various monuments (the fine theatre dating to the beginning of the imperial period may still be admired today); and modelled its town plan on those of Roman origin, laying out a series of almost parallel thoroughfares which probably constituted the basis for the subsequent medieval town plan.

On the decline and fall of the Roman Empire, Iguvium, whose name had by now been corrupted into Agobbio, suffered numerous invasions and repeated destruction at the hands of the barbarian peoples who for various centuries, in successive waves, penetrated, and devastated, the Italian peninsula. But the town always managed to recover. Its complete and definitive rebirth and reconstruction took place at the beginning of the 12th century, under the guidance and promotion of the bishop Ubaldo Baldassini (St. Ubaldus), as already noted.

The town then became a free Commune: it was the beginning of a splendid period in Gubbio's history both from the political and social, and from the cultural and artistic viewpoint. It was then that its finest public buildings and most beautiful churches were erected; that all its houses and streets gradually assumed the character that still distinguishes the town today; and that flourishing schools of painting, pottery, stone-cutting and manuscript illumination were developed.

Its power and political influence increased considerably, so much so that it succeeded progressively in asserting and consolidating its own independence, so the point not only of achieving a coalition of eleven neighbouring Communes (and in this the reputedly miraculous intervention of St. Ubaldus, later proclaimed saviour and patron of the town, was considered decisive), but also of extending its rule well beyond the confines of its own territory. A measure of this growing importance and prestige is the number of its inhabitants: 50,000, a really surprising number for those times.

In the second half of the 15th century Gubbio lost its independence as a free Commune. It was subjected first to the lordship of the Gabrielli family, and then, for a brief period, fell under the rule of Albornoz, the papal legate. On recovering its independence following a popular rising, the people of Gubbio, in order not to succumb anew to the seigneurial regime of the Gabrielli, preferred to turn instead to the powerful dukes of Montefeltro, who ruled over Urbino, and to entrust to them the administration and rule of the town.

Later, Gubbio fell into the hands of the Della Rovere family, by whom it was ruled until 1624. Then, on the death of the last heir of the Della Rovere dynasty, it was annexed to the Papal State, of which it continued to form part till its annexation to the Kingdom of Italy in 1860. From then on the history of Gubbio became identified with that of the Nation.

Worth recalling is the tragic episode that occurred at the end of the Second World War, when 40 innocent citizens of Gubbio were killed by the Nazis in reprisal for an action in the partisan war.

Many sons of Gubbio have won a niche for themselves in history, especially in the artistic field.

We may recall, first, the artist whom Dante called "l'onor d'Agobbio" (i.e. the glory, the honour of Gubbio): this was Oderisi, who lived in the mid-13th century and was particularly distinguished as a miniaturist. Especially conspicuous in the architectural field were Giovanni da Gubbio, the architect among other things of the magnificent Cathedral of Assisi, and Il Gattapone, who lived in the 14th century and designed the bridge known as the Ponte delle Torri at Spoleto and other important buildings, including, perhaps, the Palazzo dei Consoli at Gubbio itself.

The roll-call of the painters of Gubbio is a long one: Palmerucci, Ottaviano and Tommaso Nelli, and Sinibaldo Ibi, just to cite a few of the greatest. Nor should we forget distinguished stone-cutters and wood-carvers such as the members of the Maffei family and all those potters who have given glory and fame to the art of ceramics in every age. Among these latter special mention should be made of Master Giorgio, who invented and applied the technique of "reverberation", thanks to which the pottery produced by him acquired exceptional gracefulness and preciousness. Unfortunately, the technique in question was subsequently forgotten, only to be rediscovered much later (in the 19th century), when skilled potters succeeded in rediscovering its secret and thus resuming production of a type of pottery which still characterizes this particular handicraft of the town.

Yet the son of Gubbio who has surely been best known and most loved through the ages belongs not to the field of art, but to the history of the town itself and its traditions: namely, St. Ubaldus, Gubbio's patron saint.

Ubaldo Baldassini was born in Gubbio in 1105 (the house in which he was born now houses the Centre of Umbrian Studies). He became the town's bishop in 1128. But he was not only its spiritual guide: Ubaldo himself defended its independence from the assaults of both the emperor Frederick Barbarossa and a coalition of eleven other Communes; it was he who encouraged and instigated the reconstruction of the town after it had almost completely been destroyed by fire and devastation. His tireless endeavour on behalf of the town, his charismatic personality and his undoubted role as a steadfast and reliable leader, all concurred to make him a much-loved citizen, so much so that he was canonized only thirty years after his death in 1160 and proclaimed the patron saint of Gubbio.

He rests in the Basilica of Sant'Ubaldo on Monte Ingino; his body, though not embalmed, has remained intact through the centuries and is still an object of veneration by the people. It is in his honour that the annual "Corsa dei Ceri" (Race of the Candles) is run.

*Palazzo dei Consoli*

For centuries the Via dei Consoli has been Gubbio's main street. Rather wider than the typical medieval streets of the town, it winds up in gradual ascent along the flanks of Monte Ingino and leads into the Piazza della Signoria, the historical and artistic centre of the town.

# The Palazzo dei Consoli

Powerful, majestic, elegant and solemn, the Palazzo dei Consoli dominates the whole town. With its huge bulk rising massively from the Piazza Grande, it provides, even from afar, an unmistakeable point of reference in the panorama of the town.

Together with the Palazzo Pretorio and the piazza onto which they face, it was commissioned by the Magistrates of Gubbio in 1321: the whole complex was designed to act as a connecting link between the quarters of the town and to constitute its new monumental political and historic centre. The project was a daring one, because the area on which it was to arise was restricted, irregular and precipitous. The architectural solution to the problem of how best to exploit the site was, however, an extremely ingenious one: the essence of the plan was to coordinate the two buildings - the Palazzo dei Consoli and the Palazzo Pretorio - by means of a hanging piazza and to compensate for the unevenness of the terrain by massive supporting arches to buttress the buildings and the piazza itself.

The Palazzo dei Consoli represents one of the finest examples of the civil architecture of the Middle Ages and, in beauty and elegance, is rivalled by few others in Italy.

The attribution of the architect responsible for its construction is uncertain: some scholars attribute it to Angelo da Orvieto , whose name is inscribed over the entrance; others argue that this architect only designed the staircase; while others again refer the building's overall design to Matteo di Giovannello known as Il Gattapone, a native-born architect of Gubbio who was certainly no newcomer to daring creations of this kind.

Built in the Romanesque style with some features anticipating gothic and with a certain spatial arrangement which even presages the architectural forms of the Early Renaissance, the Palazzo dei Consoli is in the shape of a massive oblong structure. The façade overlooking the piazza is pierced by a large portal placed at the top of a broad and harmonious stairway. The external surfaces are articulated by four half-columns. In the upper part is a series of framed windows and, higher up still, above a row of hanging arches, is a machicolated roofline formed by a pronounced crenellation. To the left of the façade is the tall bell-tower containing the ancient bell weighing 2500 kilos.

The other sides of the building are similar to the façade with the exception of that facing onto the Via Baldassini; this is characterized by the massive buttresses on which the building rests and by the open balcony from which fine panoramic views of the town can be enjoyed.

*Via dei Consoli*
*Palazzo dei Consoli*

# The interior of the Palazzo dei Consoli

Before entering the building, we should note the fresco by Bernardino di Nanni placed in the lunette over the doorway depicting the "Madonna and Child with St. John and St. Ubaldus" and, especially, the vernacular inscription (a rather rare example of this) indicating the date of the beginning of the work.

On making our way through the entrance, we enter a large Hall (**Salone**), striking for its simplicity, imposing in its mighty proportions (it occupies the whole ground floor) and evocative in its memories of the past. It was here that the fiery assemblies of the people were held at the time when Gubbio was a free and independent Commune; it was here that the medieval Consuls harangued the citizens assembled in the piazza below from the little windows.

Apart from an interesting fresco of the "Madonna and Child with Saints" by Nelli, a number of archaeological finds and documentation of various nature are displayed in the Hall: these include various inscriptions dating both to the Roman and medieval periods, and various sarcophagi. Particularly noteworthy specimens of the latter include the Late Byzantine one dating to the 8th century, the Umbrian one and the Roman one.

The coats of arms of the civic Guilds and also the communal measures are placed along the walls of the hall. Also on display are various marble sculptures and fragments of masonry recovered from the excavations of Gubbio's Roman theatre and from other buildings of the medieval period. The hall is further embellished with a large and elegant fireplace and two beautiful carved doorways removed from the Ducal Palace.

From the main Hall we enter the **Museum of the Palazzo dei Consoli**. Here, apart from a rich collection of coins from Gubbio and Umbria, prints and some paintings, are displayed the celebrated "Eugubine Tablets". These constitute the richest and most significant documentation of the ancient civilization of the Umbri and, as such, are of enormous importance for all scholars of the period.

Consisting of seven bronze tablets dating to the 3rd century B.C., they were discovered in 1440, perhaps in the town's Roman theatre, or perhaps at Scheggia and later sold to the municipality of Gubbio. Written in the ancient Umbrian language and simultaneously in Latin and Etruscan, they describe rites, religious ceremonies and feasts of the area, and at the same time provide valuable information on the topography and distribution of the town and the subdivision of its inhabitants (called "ikuvini") according to their livelihoods.

Irrespective of their content (which is undeniably important), what is especially interesting about the tablets is their value both as an historical document testifying to the existence of ancient "Ikuvins" - Gubbio's distant progenitor - and more particularly as a linguistic document testifying to the language of the Umbrian people; in fact, they represent the most significant and most complete written source concerning the ancient civilization of the Umbri and hence the only possibility of reading and interpreting that language and confronting it with others.

*Eugubine Tablets*

*Opposite page:*
*The Palace of Consuls - Entrance hall*
*Sarcophagus of late byzantine style*

# The Palazzo dei Consoli: the Picture Gallery

The Picture Gallery (**Pinacoteca**) is situated on the upper floor of the Palazzo dei Consoli and is reached by means of the ancient stone staircase, now covered in wood to protect it from the wear and tear of time.

**Room 1**: paintings mainly dating to the 13th and 14th century are on display in the first room. They include various paintings by Palmerucci, a local artist of Gubbio who lived in the first half of the 14th century; of these particular mention may be made of a tondo depicting the "Madonna and Child with Saints Ubaldus, Marianus, John the Baptist and Jacob". The work of other artists is represented by another polyptych displayed in the room, the "Madonna and Child" by Mello and the painting representing "Jesus Crucified in the midst of Saints". Also on display in the room are a number of reliquaries, some miniatures attributable with some degree of confidence to one of the Martini brothers, and a polychrome statue of the Madonna. We may also note the handsome 16th century portal with the Montefeltro coat of arms placed against the entrance wall of the same room and a precious strong-box.

**Room 2**: works dating to the 15th century are assembled in this room. Some paintings, including the one representing "St. John", are the work of Palmerucci; others are by Mello or artists of the Umbrian school of Ottaviano Nelli or Carlo Crivelli. Particularly noteworthy is the "Pietà", an interesting work in terracotta by a German artist highly expressive for its emotionally-charged faces and the dramatic angularity of the lines of the body of Christ.

**Room 3**: artists of the 15th and 16th century are represented in this room. Worth noting is the beautiful portal in **pietra serena** (the grey stone characteristic of Florence). Of the paintings on display, special mention should be made of the "Crucifix", the small but beautiful "Madonna of the Pomegranate" attributable to Filippino Lippi or P.F. Fiorentino, and the "Madonna of Mercy" by T. Nelli in which one of Gubbio's buildings, the Ospedale dei Disciplinati, is represented. We may also note the Tabernacle with a painting attached, the finely decorated Cassone (or marriage chest) and the elegant fireplace.

**Room 4**: or Central Hall: it comprises works by local artists dating to the 15th and 16th century. The room is notable for its charming fountain at the centre and its beautiful ceiling. Apart from various paintings by Nucci and Damiani, we may mention the painting depicting "St. Ubaldus" and the "Madonna of Mercy" by Sinibaldo Ibi of the school of Perugino.

**Room 5**: works of the 16th and 17th century are assembled in this room. We may note in particular the large fresco by F. Damiani representing the episode of the wolf of Gubbio tamed by St. Francis, a painting which also includes a fine panorama of the town. The beautiful inlaid furniture and the fine fireplace are also worth noting.

**The balcony** (or **loggetta**) offers a marvellous view over the whole town.

*The Picture Gallery*
*Gonfalone of the Brotherhood of Mercy*
*with St. Ubaldus bishop and Patron of the*
*city*

*Crucifix XIV c.*

*Opposite page:*
*Central room in the Picture Gallery*
*Pietà in terracotta*

A wiew of the large room
in the Picture Gallery
Polyptych by
Guido Palmerucci

Opposite Page:
"Madonna with
Pomegranate" perhaps by
Pier Francesco Fiorentino

# The Palazzo Pretorio

The Palazzo Pretorio, now the town hall, was designed and built in conjunction with the Palazzo dei Consoli and the piazza in front, since - as explained above - the whole complex was intended by the Magistrates of the time to constitute the new and suitably imposing political and social centre of civic life. It was thus built concurrently with the other building by the architect Gattapone. But, in contrast to the latter, it was never completed, at least externally. In fact, it was intended to be similar in appearance to the Palazzo dei Consoli, and thus to constitute a twin building which would have given an impression of greater prestige and solemnity to the whole complex. However, although the Palazzo Pretorio may lack a crenellated roofline and the planned revetment of its façade, we may still recognize in it a solid architectural structure and a general plan not very dissimilar from that of the building it faces on the other side of the piazza.

The Palazzo Pretorio's bold construction, and its interplay of grand and significant volumes, may especially be seen in its interior; here, despite later alterations, we may still observe the spacious rooms characterized by very high vaults supported on engaged half-columns and especially on the solid central pillar which is the predominant motif also on the other floors.

Apart from the offices of the Municipality, the building now houses the Civic Library and Archives.

It is on the façade of the Palazzo Pretorio that the target (or "tasso" as it is called) is affixed on the occasion of the "Palio della Balestra" (Gubbio's annual Crossbow Contest).

*Palazzo Pretorio*
*XIV c. room in Palazzo Pretorio*

*Opposite page:*
*Duke's palace*
*Duke's palace - The courtyard*

# The Ducal Palace

The building of the Ducal Palace at the behest of duke Federico da Montefeltro, who was born at Gubbio, was begun in 1476, based on the more illustrious model of the Ducal Palace at Urbino. The design was probably by Laurana, but the work was completed by Francesco di Giorgio Martini.

The Ducal Palace was erected over a previous building dating back to the Middle Ages and originally the scat of the Lombard administration; it was later enlarged in the 12th century by a projecting wing resting on a series of arches commonly known as "Voltone" (i.e. large vaults).

The courtyard inside the building is particularly beautiful and harmonious, a marvellous example of a well-proportioned architectural space, serene in the perfect balance of its colonnaded arcades and wonderfully enriched by the chromatic contrast of its juxtaposition of **pietra serena** and brick. The rooms arranged around the courtyard, embellished with elegant fireplaces, are equally interesting.

# The Cathedral

The Cathedral (**Duomo**) stands in the upper part of the town in the environs of the Ducal Palace. Its façade looks onto a small and picturesque piazza, while its left flank, supported by tall buttresses, rises obliquely along the Via Sant'Ubaldo.

Gothic in style, the Cathedral dates to the second half of the 13th century. It was built on the site where a small Romanesque church, erected under the patronage of St. Ubaldus, after the middle of the 12th century, had previously existed. All that survives of this original church are the architectural remains placed to the right of the façade and the bas-reliefs of the Four Evangelists and the Lamb of God which still adorn the front of the Cathedral, arranged round a very simple rose window.

**INTERIOR OF THE CATHEDRAL**. The impression one has on entering the Cathedral is particularly striking. The broad single nave, without aisles, appears solemn and majestic with its succession of ten huge gothic arches which seem to direct the visitor's gaze upwards, with mystical force, and towards the sanctuary, to the back of which a stained glass window high in the wall diffuses light throughout the whole church.

The architecture is typical of the churches of Gubbio, but here its effect is particularly interesting and striking.

The Cathedral contains the tombs of Saints Marianus and Giacomo, remains of frescoes dating to the 13th and 14th century, a Roman sarcophagus on which the high altar rests, subsequently surrounded and decorated with gothic colonnettes, the modern stained glass in the sanctuary, two decorated organs and the Episcopal Throne carved by G. Maffei.

THE EPISCOPAL THRONE. A wonderful example of carving and inlaying, the Episcopal Throne is the work of G. Maffei (16th century). Situated in the choir of the Cathedral, it was conceived as an architectural structure: two columns finely decorated with floral motifs support a round arch.

THE STAINED GLASS IN THE APSE. The luminous stained-glass window in the Cathedral apse is of modern production. It portrays Saints Ubaldus, Marianus and Giacomo. It is to the latter two, whose relics and mortal remains are preserved here, that the Cathedral is in fact dedicated.

# The Cathedral Museum

The Cathedral Museum contains a small but valuable collection of church furnishings and paintings of various kind.

Special mention should be made of the Pluvial (or cope) of Pope Marcellus: this is a masterpiece of 16th century Flemish art. Finely woven in gold and silk, the pluvial is decorated with wonderfully embroidered scenes from the Passion of Christ. It was donated to Pope Marcellus II, by whom it was donated in turn to the town of Gubbio whose Bishop he had previously been.

The Museum also contains stone statues dedicated to Saints Marianus and Giacomo dating to the 13th century.

The "Madonna of Valdichiascio" (Cathedral Museum).

Various frescoes and paintings are displayed in the same museum. Among the most interesting, we should mention Mello da Gubbio's "Madonna and Child Enthroned flanked by Angels" and the "Madonna of Valdichiascio", a delicate painting of considerable value by the same local artist.

Many of the other works on display have survived in a much deteriorated condition, but are nonetheless of importance in the history of art of the town.

**The Crucifix**. Another of the Museum's prize exhibits is the Crucifix, a work of great refinement and preciousness both due to the material used and the mastery with which it was carved: the Christ on the cross is in fact sculpted from ivory. The work dates to the 16th century.

*Cathedral*

*Opposite page:*
*Cathedral Museum*
*Madonna of Valdichiascio*
*"Pluvial" of Pope Marcellus*

# The Basilica of Sant'Ubaldo

Much venerated by the people of Gubbio, since it preserves the body of St. Ubaldus, the much-loved patron saint of the town, the Basilica is situated high up on the slopes of Monte Ingino and is the final goal of the annual "Corsa dei Ceri". It may be reached either by the streets that wind up trough Gubbio's historic town centre, or by an easier panoramic road, or by the funicular railway.

Built in the 16th century under the patronage of the duchesses of the Della Rovere house, the church occupies the site of a more ancient building, whither the body of the Saint was removed in 1194.

The entrance-way and the cloisters preceding the church are particularly beautiful. The interior consists of a nave and two aisles on either side; it is chiefly remarkable for housing the mortal remains of Gubbio's patron saint, preserved in an urn (the work of local artists), and the famous "Candles", the huge octagonal structures carried at top speed up to the church on the occasion of the annual "Corsa dei Ceri".

# The Roman Theatre

The Theatre is situated on the outskirts of the town, in the plain facing Monte Ingino, and although it has been subjected - especially in the Middle Ages - to repeated spoliation, it still represents a monument of undoubted beauty and interest, both due to the grandeur of its proportions and the harmoniousness of its forms.

The Theatre's original construction probably dates back to the 1st century B.C., but in its present form it is to be attributed to the early years of the 1st century A.D., as is attested by a dedicatory inscription which names G. Satrius Rufus as the sponsor of the restoration.

The Theatre was of considerable size: it is enough to note that the **cavea** - or semicircular auditorium - had a diameter of 70 metres and could contain over 15,000 spectators. Apart from its stage and **scena**, the whole of the theatre's raked auditorium is still visible today; at least 22 of its stone rows of seats are still perfectly preserved. Arranged in a semicircle and interrupted by access corridors, they rest on a massive architectural structure which may be better observed from behind, and which consists of a double storey of ponderous arches; the lower one is fairly intact, but the upper one has only survived in part. We may also note that the theatre was at one time completely faced by a stone revetment which undoubtedly gave an impression of greater solemnity and importance. During the Middle Ages, much of this facing material was spoliated to provide building materials for other buildings in the town.

At the present time, performances of considerable artistic interest, notably open-air theatre, are staged in this theatre during the summer.

*Basilica of Sant'Ubaldo*
*Interior*

*Opposite page:*
*The Cloister*
*Roman Theatre*

The Piazza Quaranta Martiri, point of confluence of the various roads converging on Gubbio from its surrounding Region, constitutes the main entrance to the town. Large and irregular, it is situated beyond the ancient circuit of walls which surround the town and opens up fine panoramic views of the austere monuments clinging to the steep slopes of Monte Ingino. Named after the 40 citizens of Gubbio who were shot by the Germans in 1944 and to whom a Mausoleum has also been dedicated to commemorate their sacrifice in a worthy fashion, the Piazza is delimited by the complex of buildings forming part of the Convent of San Francesco and by the church of the same name, by the characteristic Loggia dei Tiratori and by the lively and much-frequented public gardens.

A war memorial commemorating the citizens of Gubbio killed in the First World War also stands in the Piazza; it was sculpted in travertine and bronze by Enrico Cagianelli.

# The church of San Francesco

The church of San Francesco has been attributed to the architect Fra Bevignate of Perugia, but the attribution is surrounded by many uncertainties. It is known, however, that the building of the church, begun in the mid-12th century, was completed in 1292 and that the bell-tower was only finished several years later.

The church's structure is characterized by a mixed Romanesque and Gothic style.

The monastic complex adjoining the church was built over the house and warehouse of the Spadalonga family (some remains of which are still visible) who, in the early years of the 13th century, welcomed St. Francis and gave him hospitality. This was after the saint had renounced worldly goods and stripped himself of his rich vestments in order to don nothing but a poor tunic which, according to tradition, was given to him by the Spadalonga family. It was this same tunic that would subsequently become the typical Franciscan habit.

Along its flank facing onto the Piazza Quaranta Martiri, the church presents a fine double portal surmounted by an elegant rose window. The façade and main entrance to the church are situated, however, on the opposite side to the apses, and present a rather damaged and incomplete appearance as a result of work carried out in the 18th century.

# The Loggia dei Tiratori

The building which runs along the whole of one side of the Piazza Quaranta Martiri is characterized by its long double portico surmounted by a pronounced porch roof. The lower portico rests on columns and dates to the 14th century; the upper one rests on pilasters and is a later addition.

It was here, in this Loggia, that the woolworkers, i.e. those belonging to the medieval Guild of the art of Wool, washed and dried their fabrics after they had been woven and dyed.

Famous in its time for the high quality of its cloth, the Loggia represents today one of the few buildings of its type to have survived; it is well preserved and one of the biggest of its kind.

At the present time, a fruit and vegetable market is held under the arches of the lower portico.

In a niche built into the Loggia is a fresco by Bernardino di Nanni depicting the "Madonna and Child with Saints Peter and Paul".

Here we may also find one of the entrances to the church of Santa Maria dei Laici (or dei Bianchi), whose principal façade, simple but elegant, is situated along the left side of the Loggia. The church was built at the beginning of the 14th century. Its interior, in part reconstructed, contains various frescoes, of which those in the crypt are especially notable.

# The church of San Giovanni

The church of San Giovanni dates to the 13th century and was perhaps built on the site of the ancient Cathedral of Gubbio.

The gabled façade is decorated with hanging arches; a flight of steps leads up to the broad portal. The church is flanked by a tall and massive bell-tower.

The interior consists of a single nave, surmounted by powerful arches which constitute, together with the polygonal apses, the main characteristic of Gubbio's gothic churches, of which this represents the prototype.

The walls of the church are embellished with paintings by local artists such as Nucci and Beni and by an altarpiece by Ridolfi da Verona (17th century) portraying St. Charles Borromeo. Particularly interesting is the high altar built out of limestone and decorated with elegant columns.

# The Palazzo del Bargello

The Palazzo del Bargello, so called because it was the seat of the "Bargello", or head of police in the Middle Ages, overlooks, with its severe but elegant façade, the square of the same name.

This 14th century building is a particularly handsome and typical example of Gubbio's civil architecture. It consists of three storeys divided by string-courses. Its external surfaces are finely ashlared. The windows are austere but elegant; particularly graceful is the one located between the two doors of the ground floor. The "door of the dead", situated above a short flight of steps, is very well preserved.

**THE FONTANA DEI MATTI**. This fountain (literally "The Fountain of the Mad") stands in front of the Palazzo del Bargello in the piazza of the same name. Erected in the 16th century, it consists of a basin-type fountain of simple but harmonious form.

According to a high-spirited and rather endearing local tradition, anyone who manages to make three circuits of the fountain while being splashed with water by his friends not only acquires honorary citizenship of Gubbio, but becomes a member of the happy-go-lucky company of "madmen" formed by the people of the town. "Mad", it goes without saying, in the good sense - indicating above all the refreshingly free, unconstrained, instinctive and passionate spirit that grips all the citizens of Gubbio especially at the time of their traditional annual festival, the "Corsa dei Ceri".

Church of St. Francis
The "Loggia dei Tiratori"
Church of St. John
Palazzo del Bargello and fountain of the Fools

# The Church of Sant'Agostino

The church of Sant'Agostino is situated outside the Porta Romana, a short distance beyond the town walls. Gothic in style, it was built in the mid-13th century, but the façade was remodelled in the late 19th and early 20th century.

The interior of the church consists of a single nave opened up laterally by round-arched niches, within which the various altars are placed. Here too the dominant motif of all Gubbio's ecclesiastical architecture is repeated: the large gothic arches supporting the ceiling vault.

# The Church of the Vittorina

According to tradition, the meeting between St. Francis and the wolf, and the consequent taming of the wild beast, took place close to this little church; the episode is recounted in the "Little Flowers of St. Francis". A large bronze bas-relief describing the event has been set up in commemoration.

# The Church of San Pietro

The church stands on the Piazza of the same name close to the Porta Vittoria. Its original construction dates back to a very early period, probably to the 11th century, but its architectural structure must then have been very different from what it is now. In fact the façade of the church, apart from testifying to the successive alterations to which it has been subject, shows that the original building must have been preceded by a portico, which is now completely exterior to, and abutting onto, the existing façade.

# The Church of San Francesco della Pace

The church of San Francesco della Pace (or dei Muratori, as it is sometimes called, since it was assigned, in the Middle Ages, to the Guild of Masons) was built in the 17th century in an extremely simple and austere style which still distinguishes it today. It was erected, according to tradition, on the site of the lair of the wild wolf of Gubbio tamed by St. Francis (hence the church's name) and where the beast was apparently buried. Inside, in commemoration of the event, is a statue of the Saint of Assisi amicably shaking the animal's paw and the stone on which the episode reputedly took place. We should also note the three little statues of Saints Ubaldus, George and Anthony the Abbot which are the ones placed on top of the "Candles" on the occasion of the annual "Corsa dei Ceri" on the 15 May and the three jugs dedicated to the three patron saints which are dropped to the ground to signal the start of the race.

**THE QUARTER OF SAN MARTINO**. It is the oldest quarter of Gubbio and one of its most characteristic and evocative. It extends along the banks of the river Camignano which runs through the western part of the town. The whole area presents a succession of old medieval houses, of unforgettable views: an alternation of little streets and bridges, and silent alleyways. The past seems to relive in every corner of it: it has remained indelibly marked in its every window and door, in the coats of arms of the Wool Guild which had its seat here, in the stones of the houses darkened by centuries, and above all in the atmosphere which permeates the whole quarter.

**THE PALAZZO DEL CAPITANO DEL POPOLO**. This building is an extremely fine example of 13th century civil architecture built in the style typical of other buildings of Gubbio of the same period. It consists of three storeys characterized by a handsome facing in local stone and pierced by elegant windows surmounted by pointed arches and by a loggia (on the top floor), it too with gothic arches.

The building is solid and severe in appearance, but at the same time elegant and harmonious in the clear-cut articulation of its surfaces and in its curvilinear frontage which accompanies the curve of the street itself.

In the Middle Ages, the building was the seat of the Captain of the People, an office which was of the great prestige in the communal period because it represented the highest authority in the town.

**THE VIA DEL CAPITANO DEL POPOLO**. This street, which takes its name from the building of greatest prestige to be found on it, is another typical survival of the medieval period: narrow, winding and silent, it runs between ancient houses which are still intact in character and which have acquired, in the course of the centuries, a truly unforgettable evocativeness and fascination.

Facing the entrance to the Palazzo del Capitano del Popolo, we may note a large stone slab of oval shape at the centre of the street: the stone marks the spot on which, following a centuries-old tradition, the Dead (Christ) stops to rest during the annual Good Friday procession.

*The quarter of San Martino*

*Church of Sant'Agostino - Inside*
*Church of San Pietro*
*Church of the Vittorina*
*Church of San Francesco della Pace*

# The "Corsa dei Ceri" (Race of the Candles)

Perhaps it would be superfluous to describe at any length a festival which is by now sufficiently well-known not only in Umbria (which chose the "Candles" as the device of its regional coat of arms) and Italy, but also in a large part of the world. Yet in spite of its fame, at least some attempt to describe the "Corsa dei Ceri" could hardly be avoided in a guide to Gubbio. And in making this attempt, it is not just a question of trying to penetrate and grasp its significance and historical development. For in speaking about the festival as in being a spectator at it, in watching it as in participating in it, the aim is above all to discover and interiorize the town's character, the spirit of its people, and the mysterious, total and unrestrained involvement of its whole population in an annual event which continues to revitalize its history and tradition. In describing the "Corsa dei Ceri", we must try to understand how a spirit that is centuries - if not millennia - old can be revivified each year: born anew like the phoenix, and bursting so exuberantly into suddenly renewed life in the town's streets and squares as to instil even the visitor with a kind of magic enthusiasm and excited participation.

## The origins of the festival

The fact that the "Corsa dei Ceri" belongs to a distant past makes it difficult to explain its origins, all the more so since this festival, which undoubtedly presents the character of a religious event (celebrated as it is on 15 May, the anniversary of the death of the town's patron saint St. Ubaldus), reveals, on closer examination, a number of features that are not peculiarly or exclusively Christian. It is possible in fact to identify in it not only local, folkloric features of the Early Middle Ages, but even links with ancient pagan rites associated with spring, and with the fertility of the earth, and thus with festivals in honour of the goddess of agriculture, Ceres. Some scholars, indeed, argue that it was from the name of this goddess that the term "Ceri" (in Italian: candles) derives, and that these latter, which are far from being big candles as the name would suggest, but huge wooden constructions, are the result of the transformations undergone in the process of time by ancient phallic symbols.

It would seem, therefore, that the religious festival celebrated in the "Corsa dei Ceri" was grafted onto these survivals of rituals of rustic origin connected with the cycle of the seasons and the fertility of the fields. This religious festival was instituted, at the behest of the people of Gubbio themselves, after 1154, the year in which the bishop of the town Ubaldo Baldassini, thanks to his reputedly miraculous intervention, saved Gubbio from a coalition formed of a number of hostile Communes. In commemoration of his action, the citizens of Gubbio wanted to establish a festival which would recall the event and honour the saviour of their town. Yet it was a festival that initially took a different form than it does now: it consisted perhaps of a procession of the faithful up to the tomb of the Saint (probably bearing candles in their hands); it certainly consisted of the tribute annually brought by the various guilds of the town. Year after year, however, its character changed, and the race, the rituals and customs that characterize the festival today gradually took shape.

What has undoubtedly remained unaltered over the centuries is the profound, all-embracing and passionate involvement of the population of Gubbio in the event: their very civic identity is expressed and glorified by it.

Another demonstration of the spirit with which the festival is celebrated is the fact that, during the World War, in the absence of menfolk, it was the women of Gubbio themselves who ran the race.

The "Corsa dei Ceri" is held on the 15 May each year. The "Ceri" (literally: candles) carried in the race are huge wooden constructions, approximately 7 metres high, and in the shape of two octagonal prisms. They are respectively surmounted on top by images of St. Ubaldus, patron saint of the town and protector of masons; St. George, protector of merchants; and St. Anthony, protector of peasants and students (these various categories of workers can be traced back to the ancient medieval guilds). To enable these heavy octagonal constructions to be carried in a race through the town and up the steep slopes of Monte Ingino, they are supported on wooden platforms with projecting beams by which the "ceraioli" - as the bearers of the "Candles" are called - are able to support them on their shoulders.

The bearers all wear distinctive traditional costumes for the race, consisting of a hat, shirt, trousers, scarf round the waist and neckerchief. But these vary in colour according to the Saint to whom they belong: the shirt being yellow for St. Ubaldus, blue for St. George and black for St. Anthony.

## The programme of the festival

**1st Sunday in May**: the "Candles", which remain enclosed in the Basilica of Sant'Ubaldo for the whole year, are brought down to the town in the midst of a festive crowd.

**15 May, in the morning**: the Captains (those in charge of the running of the festival) and the so-called "Capodieci" (or foremen, of which there are three, each in charge of one of the three "Candles"), on being awoken by the sound of trumpets, make their way, together with the "ceraioli", to the church of San Francesco della Pace or dei Muratori, where they attend Mass, remove the statuettes of the three Saints kept there and, on marching in procession to the Palazzo dei Consoli, place them on top of the "Candles".

Later, they receive the homage of a bunch of flowers from girls in costume in the church of Santa Lucia.

**11.00 a.m.**: procession of all the participants in the event to the Piazza della Signoria.

**12.00 a.m.**: to the sound of the pealing of the town-bell, the so-called "raising of the Candles" takes place amidst general rejoicing. This is accompanied by a precise ritual and the custom of smashing three jugs of water as a kind of augury for the good outcome of the race. The "Candles" are then borne in procession through the town, before being laid in a horizontal position, one behind the other, in the Via Savelli della Porta.

**15 May, 6.00 p.m.**: this is the culminating moment of the festival. It begins with a renewed lifting of the "Candles" which, on the arrival of the procession and their blessing by the Bishop, then start their frenetic race through the streets of the town. Such is their weight that the "ceraioli" - supporting on their shoulders the poles on which the "Candles" rest - are, once they are exhausted by the enormous effort, continually relieved by relays of new bearers.

On returning to the Piazza della Signoria, on a signal from the Mayor, they perform three helter-skelter circuits of the piazza, and then rush off at full tilt to

*The raising of the candles*

ascend the precipitous streets up the slopes of Monte Ingino to the Basilica of Sant'Ubaldo. The race is over, the door of the church is closed: the "ceraioli" inside it, in a final rite, drum loudly on the sides of their "Candles" with their hands.

The festival of the "Ceri" is thus completed, and the "Candles" remain deposited in the basilica until the following year.

The whole race takes place in the space of just a few minutes: all the sheer effort, skill and euphoria is concentrated into a small, but correspondingly intense, space of time. But the actual race does not exhaust the fascination of the event. The hearts of the people of Gubbio still throb with the emotion of the race, its progress, the raising of the "Candles", their circuits and terrible swayings. And it is now that the discussions begin about who was the winner. The way of establishing which of the three "Candles" has won is indeed very curious. For it is not a question of who arrives first: they always run in exactly the same order - first St. Ubaldus, second St. George and third St. Anthony. Nor is it possible for them to overtake each other, both due to the narrowness of the streets, and due to the rules of the game which have been established for centuries. The winner is considered the "Candle" that succeeds in most increasing the distance between it and the one behind or in closing the gap between it and the one in front, to the point of actually resting its poles on it or even closing the doors of the Basilica before the arrival of the following "Candle".

# The "Palio della Balestra" (Crossbow Contest)

Apart from the more celebrated "Corsa dei Ceri", another folkloric event is annually held in Gubbio. It too boasts of very ancient origins and re-evokes aspects of the life and history of the far-off Middle Ages in costume, arms, emblems and methods of combat. This is the "Palio della Balestra" (Crossbow Contest): a contest of skill and precision between the most able crossbowmen of the town and those of Borgo San Sepolcro, a town in neighbouring Tuscany.

The competition is disputed on two occasions: first in Gubbio on the last Sunday of May, and then in Borgo San Sepolcro in September. It consists of shooting projectiles by crossbow from a fixed position at a target (known as the "tasso") which is mounted on the façade of the Palazzo Pretorio (the town hall) in the Piazza della Signoria. The crossbows in question, which are still made in Gubbio, thus enriching the wide range of ancient handicrafts which still flourishingly survive in the town, were used since the time of the Crusades and constituted a fearsome weapon. Companies of crossbowmen were indeed formed in various Italian towns, specialized in the training of troops in the use of the crossbow; companies which in some cases, as in that of Gubbio, continued to survive even after the invention of gunpowder had rendered certain methods of combat obsolete.

It was at this point that people began to organize contests in which they could continue to exercise the ancient art of warfare and display their own fighting skills.

Yet a suggestive image of Gubbio is the biggest tree in the world, raised in 1981 by a group of devotees of the Basilica of Sant'Ubaldo. Situated on Monte Ingino, on which the Basilica of Sant'Ubaldo (Patron Saint of Gubbio) stands, the tree is 350 metres high and is formed of 12 km of electrical cables and illuminated by 450 bulbs.

*Birate*
*The race of the candles*
*Palio of the Crossbow*
*The biggest tree in the world*

# Orvieto

An important Etruscan town, identified by some with Volsinii veteres (or also Urbivetus, old town, in contradistinction to Volsinii-novi, the neighbouring Bolsena), Orvieto also maintained its thriving economy in Roman times, based especially on the production of pottery.

During the barbarian invasions, Orvieto was occupied by Alaric and Odoacer. Vitigis, in turn, exploited its strong natural position to turn it into a defensive bastion in his war against the Byzantines under Belisarius, who succeeded in conquering it after a stubbornly-resisted siege in 538. Temporarily reoccupied by Totila before the final Gothic defeat, Orvieto was later occupied by the Lombard Agilulf in 596. The town was granted its own bishop and, in 606, its own counts. A count of Orvieto, Farolf, as part of the religious revival promoted by the emperor Otto III, cooperated with St. Romuald in fostering the foundation of abbeys and monasteries in the surrounding territory.

In the 11th-12th century Orvieto set itself up as a Commune. The first towers, tower-houses and mansions of the nobility that moved from the countryside into the town began to arise. The Commune later rebelled against the papal governors installed to control it and engaged in lengthy struggles until it was finally recognised by Pope Hadrian IV.

By 1137 Orvieto had already become an independent city-state and speedily became a prominent Guelph stronghold in Central Italy, fighting off the repeated attacks of Ghibelline exiles and the Hohenstaufen emperors Frederick I and Henry IV. The papal nomination of the first "podestà" (chief magistrate), the Roman Pietro Parenzo, dates to 1199; he was later killed during the internecine strife between the opposing factions of the Monaldeschi (Guelphs) and Filippeschi (Ghibellines) which continued unabated throughout the 13th century.

In 1281-84, the French Pope Martin IV established himself in Orvieto, filling the town with his own fellow-citizens, against whom the people rebelled. On the rekindling of civil strife, the Filippeschi were expelled from the town in August 1313, but their rivals, the Monaldeschi, became themselves divided into the opposing Beffati and Malcorini factions. In 1334 civil unrest was quelled by Ermanno Monaldeschi della Cervara, who became Orvieto's first Lord and ruled it until his death in 1337. A few years later, in 1354, Cardinal Albornoz occupied the town and annexed it to the papal state. Orvieto, however, preserved its communal institutions and liberties. In the following centuries it combined a measure of independence with the dignity of capital of the fifth province of the papal state, one it retained until 1798.

After the Napoleonic interlude, Orvieto was incorporated in the delegation of Viterbo and in 1831 once again became capital of the province until being annexed to the Italian State in 1860.

Many archaeological remains testify to the existence of Etruscan and Roman monuments in the town and its immediate environs. Of the town's surviving medieval heritage, many fortified town-houses and several churches testify to the Romanesque style. The Gothic style - initially combined with the Romanesque - begins to emerge in the mid-13th century. It was during this period that Orvieto gave birth to the mastermason Master Angelo, the builder of the Palazzo Pubblico in Città di Castello and the Palazzo dei Consoli in Gubbio.

Orvieto's biggest piazza is the Piazza del Popolo. It is dominated by the imposing Palazzo del Capitano del Popolo, on which particular beauty is conferred by the warm golden colour assumed over the centuries by the soft volcanic stone (tufa) with which it is entirely built. Originally built as a papal palace during the pontificate of Hadrian IV (ca. 1157), it is in the Orvietan Romanesque-Gothic style and consists of an open loggia on the ground floor and a large council-hall on the first floor. Later the Church granted it to the Commune as the seat of the Captain of the People. And to make it habitable on the eastern side, above the triumphal staircase, a room (called the "Caminata") was added, its exterior imitating the motif of the round triple-arched mullioned windows of the large hall. In 1280, furthermore, a bell-tower was added at the building's eastern end, while to the west the council hall was altered to give it its present appearance. Following the subsequent closure of the arcades of the ground floor loggia, the two pointed arches were opened to form the so-called "Arco della Pesa". A modern restoration carried out by the architects Paolo and Carlo Zampi has restored the building to its original appearance.

*The Palazzo Comunale*
*Palace of the Captain of the People*

*Opposite page:*
*The Cathedral*

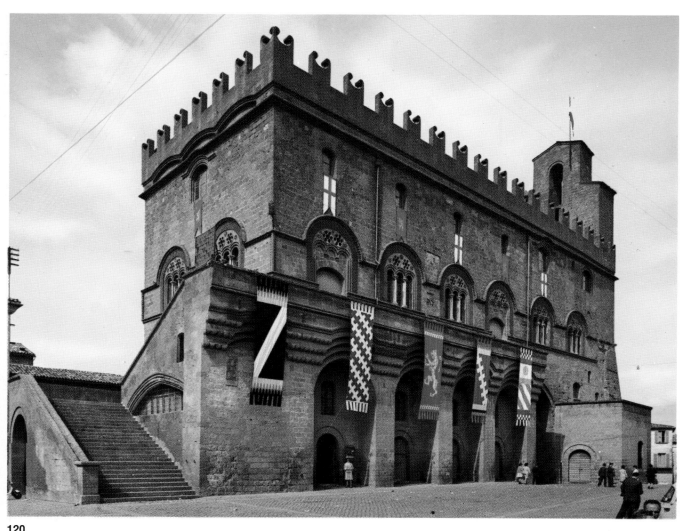

# The Cathedral

In 1263/4 a Bohemian priest - a certain Peter of Prague - incredulous about the transubstantiation of the Body of Christ in the Host and the Wine, went on a pilgrimage to Rome to pray on the tomb of St. Peter for the strengthening of his faith. On the return journey from Rome, he stopped at Bolsena where, on celebrating Mass in the Crypt of Santa Cristina, he saw blood dripping from the Host, so much so that the Caporal - the eucharistic altar cloth - was quite soaked with it.

Pope Urban IV, who was then in Orvieto, was so impressed by this miraculous event that he ordered the linen cloth to be transported there and later established the Feast of Corpus Christi for the whole Christian world. The clergy and people agreed that a worthy shrine should be built to house the Relic. And on 13 November 1290 Pope Nicholas IV laid the foundation stone of the new church. The place chosen for it was the one already occupied by the churches of San Costanzo and Santa Maria Prisca. Work on the construction of the Cathedral was protracted for roughly three centuries. The first architect was probably Arnolfo di Cambio: to him has also been attributed the design for a single - gabled façade preserved in the Cathedral Museum. It seems, however, that the first master mason responsible for the Cathedral's construction was Fra Bevignate da Perugia who built the nave and side aisles.

The work was then continued by a local builder, Giovanni Uguccione, who introduced the Gothic style in the crossing and the apse. Right from the outset, however, the stability of the Cathedral's principal load-bearing structures was in doubt, with the result that it was decided to call in an expert to give his view.

The Sienese architect and sculptor Lorenzo Maitani was the man chosen. He not only ensured the stability of the dangerous transepts by the buttresses he himself designed (1309-10), but delighted the citizens of Orvieto with his coloured design for a triple-gabled façade to the new church. With the construction of the façade he also began and pursued that of the roof.

Before his death, Maitani had left his architectural impress not only on the façade, but also on the interior of the church, such as the construction of the tribune over the wings of the eastern buttresses, a masterpiece of elegance and harmony which he completed by his Gothic transformation of the Sanctuary.

The building of the tribune was finished after Maitani's death in Orvieto in June 1330.

## THE INTERIOR OF THE CATHEDRAL

Vast, simple and austere, the interior of the Cathedral combines the most precious elements of Lombard art. On entering this great basilica, the visitor is immediately struck by its spaciousness, the perspective effect of its massive columns, and its characteristic decoration in striped white and green marbles.

The Cathedral's monumental organ, one of the biggest in Italy, was placed in the left transept, over the wall in which the entrance of the Cappella del Corporale is situated. The magnificent organ-case was designed by the 16th century Orvietan artist Ippolito Scalza; the wooden ornaments were carved by Ercole Urbani and Gianni Carpentieri, while the instrument itself was produced by Bernardino Benvenuti. After undergoing various modifications in 1913, the organ was subjected to further work of maintenance and consolidation in 1975.

## THE CAPPELLA DEL CORPORALE

The left aisle leads, at the end of the transept, into the Chapel named after the Corporal (chalice-cloth) of the Miracle of Bolsena: the relic which is preserved in a reliquary over the principal altar.

## THE RELIQUARY OF THE CORPORAL

It is the most important and precious work preserved in Orvieto Cathedral, and at the same time one of the greatest masterpieces of Sienese and Italian goldsmith's work. Commissioned from the goldsmith Ugolino di Vieri by the Bishop of Orvieto, Beltramo Monaldeschi, in 1337, the reliquary was probably completed in December 1339, the year in which the final payment of the work was made. The silver-gilt reliquary, resembling in form the façade of the Cathedral, is 1.39 m. high and 0.63 m. broad; it contains the sacred chalice-cloth of the Miracle of Bolsena. The surfaces of the reliquary are decorated with scenes in transparent enamel recounting episodes from the Miracle of Bolsena and the Life of Christ.

## THE CAPPELLA NUOVA OR CHAPEL OF THE MADONNA DI S. BRIZIO

The construction of the Cappella Nuova - later called the Chapel of the Madonna di San Brizio when the miraculous image of the Madonna of the same name was placed there - was decided by the Cathedral Board of Works in 1397. The decoration of the Chapel, after lengthy negotiations with some of the leading artists of the time, including Perugino, was finally assigned to Luca Signorelli, who requested and obtained 575 ducats, of which one part in kind (wheat and wine), as well as a house. Signorelli began work on the Chapel's frescoes on 5 April 1499.

His first task was to proceed to the completation of the two vaults begun a half century earlier by Fra Angelico and Benozzo Gozzoli.

Signorelli succeeded in recapturing the chromatic tones employed by his predecessors, while at the same time imbuing them with his own personality and art. He worked on the Chapel's frescoes with great dedication for approximately two years; his mural paintings comprise representations of "Stories of the Antichrist", "The Last Judgement", "The Resurrection of the Flesh", "The Damned", "The Blessed", "The Condemned descending into Hell" and "The Blessed ascending into Heaven".

The lower part of the Chapel's walls are decorated with arabesques and medallions of illustrious men, surrounded by scenes from ancient poetry.

The theme originally chosen for the decoration of the Chapel - probably on the advice of some Orvietan theologians - was the Last Judgement, a recurrent one in 14th century Italian art. Signorelli's representation of the Last Judgement consists of a series of independent scenes, combined with the doings of the "Antichrist", "The Prophecies" and "The Destruction of the World".

*Inside of the Cathedral*

# The Cathedral Museum
# The Palazzo Soliano

The Papal Palace (the Palazzo dei Papi), also known as the Palazzo Soliano, after the name of the district in which it is situated, stands to the right of the Cathedral.

Today, the Cathedral Museum (the Museo dell'Opera del Duomo) is housed in the frontal wing of the building. At the centre of the large hall on the first floor panels from a polyptych by Simone Martini (1280-1344) can be admired; they represent the Madonna and Child, Saints Peter and Paul, and Saints Mary Magdalen and Domenic. The Museum also contains some splendid examples of medieval goldsmith's work, notably the reliquary of the skull of Saint Savinus (1340), a masterpiece by the Sienese goldsmiths Ugolino di Vieri and Viva di Lando. Various frescoes removed from churches in Orvieto are displayed on the entrance wall.

Against the other walls are fragments of the roof and tie beams from the Cathedral, a Madonna and Child with Saints Savinus and Giovenale, a tile frescoed with a self-portrait of Signorelli and a portrait of Nicola di Angelo Franchi, chamberlain of the Cathedral's Board of Works in 1500. The Museum also houses the designs on parchment for the façade of the Cathedral: one with only a single gable, attributed by some to Arnolfo di Cambio and by others to Maitani; the other triple-gabled and universally assigned to Maitani.

Noteworthy, too, are the Museum's holdings of works of sculpture by Sienese artists. These include works by Arnolfo di Cambio (1245-1310); Andrea Pisano (1270-1348); Michele Sanmicheli (1484-1559); Giovanni Dupré and other wooden statues of the Redeemer and a Madonna and Child, works by unknown masters of the 14th century.

# The "Claudio Faina" Archaeological Museum

The ground floor contains a fine collection of archaeological remains including objects found within the town of Orvieto itself and others recovered from the Croce del Tufo necropolis. Objects of particular interest include a tomb-stone from Croce del Tufo, a cinerary urn, the so-called Venus of Cannicella, and the polychrome sarcophagus found in the nearby village of Torre San Severo in 1912: finds which date from the 6th to the 2nd century B.C.

Memorial stones with Etruscan inscriptions and cremation urns of the Villanovan period are displayed on the first floor. Particularly fine is the collection of Etruscan *bucchero* (black pottery) dating to the 6th and 5th century B.C., vases, drinking cups, weapons and armour.

The Museum also contains numerous Black- and Red-figure vases imported from Greece and dating from 560 to 530 B.C. Apart from three large amphorae signed by EXEKIAS (second half of the 6th century B.C.), displayed in the central disply-case, there are also a number of Etruscan Red-figure vases, silver-plated vases and small Etruscan and Roman sculptures. Of the many other finds on display, the three Orvietan vases are distinguished by their stylistic details and unusual decoration.

*Palazzo Soliano - The outside*
*"Claudio Faina" Archaeological Museum - Attic amphora with black figures by the "Painter of Amasis" (550 B.C.) Vulci origin? - Valentini Bonaparte Collection*

*Opposite page:*
*The Cathedral Museum - Main hall*
*"Claudio Faina" Archaeological Museum - Main hall*

# The Pozzo di San Patrizio

From the Piazza Cahen - between the Fortezza degli Albornoz, the former funicular station and the gardens surrounding the remains of an Etruscan temple - a short tree-lined avenue leads down to the panoramic terrace where one of Orvieto's main attractions is located: the Pozzo di San Patrzio or St. Patrick's Well.

The well was sunk by Pope Clement VII (the Florentine Giulio de' Medici) during his stay in Orvieto where he had sought refuge during the Sack of Rome in December 1527. The Florentine architect Antonio da Sangallo the Younger was commissioned to carry out the work. After a suitable source of water had been located in the *Fonti di San Zero* at the foot of the rock (the immediate environs of Orvieto were once prolific in natural springs), the work was immediately begun and, during Sangallo's absences, continued under the direction of Giovan Battista da Cortona. In 1532, at a depth of 200 feet, a pre-Etruscan tomb was discovered. After the tufa seam had been dug through, the work of excavation continued through successive strata of tertiary clay, while the central shaft and well shafts were built out of tufa blocks and bricks. The well was not finished until 1537 under the pontificate of Paul III (Alessandro Farnese).

This artesian well - a formidable piece of engineering - was sunk to ensure water supplies in the event of the town being besieged. Another version about the method used in its construction has it that the excavations began from the bottom, first by digging a short lateral shaft into the rock and then continuing upwards; the excavated material then would have fallen by its own gravity and could be removed with greater simplicity.

The well, which is circular in section, is approximately 62 metres deep and 13.40 metres wide. Two diametrically opposite doors lead into two concentric spiral staircases, the one superimposed over the other, in such a way as to be independent of each other and non-communicating: thus preventing those coming up from obstructing those going down. Lit by 70 windows, each stairway consists of 248 comfortable steps, almost like a ramp, and easy to descend even for pack animals which went down to drink at the well from a wooden bridge, just above the water level, where the stairway ended, before going back up the opposite stairway. The descent of the well is a fascinating experience, both in view of its unique method of construction and the sensations it arouses: the temperature drops gradually as one descends, and the light grows less and less, and as one looks up from the little bridge at the bottom, the cylindrical shaft appears splashed with patches of blue and pale green, deriving from the vegetation which in part covers the walls.

The well, which has been visited with extraordinary curiosity ever since it was first opened in 1556, later came to be known as the "Pozzo di San Patrizio", because it was thought to resemble, albeit vaguely, the chasm which plummeted down from the Irish cave in which St. Patrick used to withdraw to pray.

An elegant Latin inscription, carved on two plaques attached to the two entrances, epitomises the reasons why this artesian well was built: "QUOD NATURA MUNIMENTO INVIDERAT INDUSTRIA ADIECIT".

The Piazza Cahen is dominated by the Fortezza dell'Albornoz. This fortress was built by the Pontifical Legate Cardinal Egidio Albornoz at the behest of Pope Innocent VI and on the instructions of the soldier-of-fortune and military engineer Ugolino di Montermarte in 1364. Damaged on several occasions, it was reconstructed immediately after the fall of Orvieto's last republican regime and the final subjection of the town to the Papal State (1450-1457).

Its inner buildings later fell into ruins,and its outer ditches were filled in during work on the construction of the funicular railway in 1888. More recently, the interior of the fortress has been laid out as a public park and the walkway round the top of its ramparts restored; from here fine views may be enjoyed of the Paglia valley with the underlying railway station, the Autostrada del Sole and Bracci's now-disused water-powered funicular, which enters the town through a tunnel dug under the fortress.

*St. Patrick's well*

*Opposite page:*
*Porta Postierla or*
*Porta della Rocca*
*Fortress or Rocca of*
*Albornoz*
*St. Patrick's well - Inside*

# Spoleto

Spoleto, the town of the Festival of Two Worlds, which with its cultural events of the highest standard annually attracts tourists from all over the world, is magnificently situated, spread out over gently-sloping hills, and dominated by its proud castle and the densely wooded slopes of Monteluco to its back. Richly endowed, as few other cities in Umbria or elsewhere in Italy are, with historic monuments, especially of the medieval period, Spoleto is an unforgettable town both for its beauty and because it has become the centre of an arts festival of international stature, as well as the venue of important study conferences, such as the annual Congress on the Early Middle Ages.

Spoleto's history is also illustrious. Founded in prehistoric times, it was occupied by the ancient Umbrians, under whom it rose to political power and economic importance. It later became a flourishing and splendid Roman town with the name of Spoletium (a name of Etruscan origin, suggesting a temporary ascendancy of Etruscan civilization over part of this territory).

After suffering under the Gothic invasions, Spoleto was occupied by the Lombards and, in the 6th century, became the capital of the Duchy of Spoleto which rapidly rose to such great political importance that its dukes aspired to the imperial crown itself. It was during the same period that the town extended its rule over the surrounding territory until a large part of Central Italy lay under its control.

Weakened by the major defeat inflicted on it by Frederick Barbarossa, Spoleto, from the 12th century onwards, was subjected to the Papal State. In the ensuing period it was torn by continuing civil strife and, in both the political and economic and social field, characterized by alternating periods of greater or lesser splendour and importance. Essentially, however, its history was not dissimilar from that of many other Umbrian towns, while maintaining, in some ways, an historically and culturally pre-eminent role.

# The Cathedral

A superb architectural masterpiece of this splendid town, the Cathedral of Santa Maria Assunta is a combination of various styles which testify to the successive phases in its construction, but which are fused together into a harmonious whole. The building in fact incorporates a number of structural components of the Roman period, as may be ascertained in its bell-tower. The main body of the church is, however, medieval, as is especially apparent in its façade, while the elegant portico in front is Renaissance in style.

The Cathedral is handsomely situated at the far end of the Piazza del Duomo and forms the backdrop to the grand concert by which Spoleto's arts festival is concluded each year. The Cathedral's façade is particularly interesting: it is divided into three vertical compartments by pilaster strips, decorated by slightly pointed arches and pierced by a number of rose-windows. At its centre, a richly ornamented portal leads into the nave of the church. Above, a large mosaic of Christ Enthroned, flanked by Mary and John, occupies the central arch of the upper storey.

The entrance to the Cathedral is preceded by an elegant portico, flanked by a tall Romanesque bell-tower.

**Interior** - A basilica in plan, it has a central nave and two aisles with six bays each. The original construction in the Romanesque style was altered by the remodelling of the interior in a late-Renaissance style by the architect Arrigucci.

Of particular interest is the pavement of the central nave, which represents one of the masterpieces of medieval cosmatesque art (inlaid with precious marbles). It is the original floor.

**Entrance Wall - Portrait of Urban VIII**, beautiful bronze bust sculpted by Bernini in 1640 and dedicated to the Pope who had been Bishop of Spoleto in the early years of the 17th century.

**Right Aisle - Eroli Chapel**: it was erected as a Baptistery in the 15th century, and is decorated with an interesting cycle of frescoes by Pinturicchio.

- **Chapel of the Assumption**: it too belonged to the Eroli family. Its Renaissance architecture is notable for its elegance, proportion and harmony. The frescoes that decorate it are mainly attributable to the 16th century.

**Right Transept - Tomb of Giovanni Francesco Orsini**, sculpted by Ambrogio Barocci in the 16th century.

- **Tomb of Fulvio Orsini**.

- **Altar**, designed by Valadier. Above it is a painting of the **Madonna and Child in Glory** by Annibale Carracci.

- **Tomb of Filippo Lippi**: the funerary monument dedicated to the great Florentine artist who died in Spoleto in 1469. The tomb was designed by his son Filippino Lippi and commissioned by Lorenzo de' Medici. Note in particular the fine portrait of the painter.

- **Chapel of the Icon**: over the Altar embellished with precious marble is the **Icon** that the emperor Frederick Barbarossa donated to the Cathedral of Spoleto.

**Apse** - This part of the Cathedral is decorated with a wonderful cycle of **frescoes of the Life of Mary** which represent the last great masterpiece of Filippo Lippi; he painted them with the assistance of another great artist of the period, Piermatteo D'Amelia.

- **Chapel of the Sacrament**: situated to the left of the apse, it dates in its architecture to the 17th and in its decoration to the 18th century.
- **Sacristy of the Chapel of the Sacrament**: it is particularly interesting because recent restoration and meticulous research have succeeded in bringing to light part of the original Romanesque structure of the ancient Cathedral.
- **Chapel of Sant'Anna**: it dates to the 14th century, but has been substantially remodelled in subsequent periods. It is decorated with paintings of various period.

**Left Transept** - Here we may note various paintings, tombs and an altar in precious marbles by Valadier.

**Left Aisle - Chapel of the Relics**, initially designed to house the Icon. Of particular interest are the magnificently carved and inlaid cabinets and a number of paintings.
- **Canons' House**, erected by Bishop Andrea in the 11th century but much altered at a later period.

The fine 16th century **Cloister** preserves its original herring-bone brick paving, and contains many sculptural fragments from the old Cathedral.

From here we may enter the splendid CRYPT OF SAN PRIMIANO, a rare example of unspoilt medieval architecture: it has a semicircular plan with a vaulted ceiling. It probably dates to the 9th century.

*Frescoes of the Apse - Birth of Christ*
*(Filippo Lippi)*
*Chapel of Relics - Altar Cross (Alberto Sozio)*

*Opposite page:*
*Frescoes of the Apse -*
*The Coronation of the Virgin, detail*
*(Filippo Lippi)*

**THE ARCH OF DRUSUS.** This wonderful Roman triumphal arch was erected in 23 A.D. in honour of Drusus, son of the Emperor Tiberius.

**THE ROMAN THEATRE** – Long buried under ground and not easily identifiable due to the various buildings that had arisen around it, it is only in recent years that it has been properly excavated and major restoration work begun in the bid to reconstitute its original structure. The theatre dates to the 1st century A.D.

**THE ROMAN AMPHITHEATRE** – It dates to the 2nd century A.D. Rather little has survived of its ancient structure, since it was transformed into a fortress in the Middle Ages and later quarried for the necessary stone with which to build the Rocca. But what remains of the amphitheatre – ten large arcades which formed part of its ambulatory – bears eloquent witness to its size and grandeur.

**THE CHURCH OF SANT'EUFEMIA** – Its entrance is situated in the courtyard of the Archbishop's Residence. A fine example of the Romanesque style, it has a simple and plain façade, while its small but well-proportioned interior is notable for its women's galleries. It also contains some valuable paintings.

**THE CHURCH OF SAN GREGORIO MAGGIORE** – Situated on the Piazza Garibaldi, it is dedicated to St. Gregory the Great who, together with other illustrious Christians, was buried here, in a chapel over which the existing church was built. It is Romanesque in style. The handsome façade is preceded by a 16th century portico and flanked by a Baptistery built out of a pre-existing chapel.

Thanks to recent restoration, the interior, too, has been restored to its original Romanesque appearance.

**The Picture-Gallery (Pinacoteca)** is housed in the Palazzo Comunale (13th century), and contains numerous paintings ranging in date from the 12th to the 17th century. The most prominent artists represented in the collection include the so-called "Master of Cesi", Niccolò di Liberatore (nicknamed l'Alunno), Giovanni di Pietro (lo Spagna), Sebastiano Conca and Guercino.

**The Gallery of Modern Art** is situated in the Convent of the Augustinians, and comprises a series of distinguished works by leading contemporary Italian painters and sculptors, including Pizzinato, Vespignani, Guttuso, Ceroli and Mafai.

**The Collection of Sacred Art**, housed in the Diocesan Palace, includes paintings by various artists, including once more the anonymous "Master of Cesi".

Lastly, the **Civic Museum (Museo Civico)** contains a display, in its various rooms, of a series of archaeologicals finds of various nature and provenance; they comprise fragments of bas-reliefs from churches, sarcophagi, funerary urns, inscriptions and cippi.

**THE BASILICA OF SAN SALVATORE.** It is situated on the outskirts of the town close to the Cemetery. It is one of the best-preserved and most interesting Early Christian churches in the region. It dates to the 4th century A.D., but was subjected to a number of alterations, especially in the Middle Ages. Recent restorations, however, have stripped the church of its later encrustations and revealed its original architecture in all its beauty. This is especially striking in its wonderful façade, in which classicizing features, Romanesque features and even traces of oriental influence are all clearly visible. The interior of the basilica, whose nave and aisles assume a decidedly vertical thrust, is notable in particular for its beautiful sanctuary and apse.

**THE CHURCH OF SAN PONZIANO.** Situated in the outskirts of Spoleto, outside the Porta Ponziana and on the other side of the river Tessino, this church and the monastic complex to which it belongs were founded, according to tradition, on the site where the young Ponziano, later to become the patron saint od

*Town Hall*

Roman Theatre
Church of St. Eufemia, the Apses
Drusus Arch

# The Caio Melisso Theatre

Many of the most magical performances of the Festival of Two Worlds are staged in the Caio Melisso Theatre.

Its origins date back to the 17th century, when a site intended for the building of a mansion-house was used instead to build a little theatre dedicated to the perfomances of comedies – Spoleto was, indeed, characterized by a long-standing and lively tradition of comic theatre and boasted among her sons a number of authors of this genre.

In the following two centuries, the theatre acquired considerable fame, so much so that Rossini staged his "Italian in Algiers" here. But in the early years of the 19th century it was stripped of much of its beautiful decoration and fell into delapidation following a fire. As a result the municipal authorities decided to build a new theatre to replace it: this was the Teatro Nuovo. Not very long afterwards, however, the reconstruction of the Caio Melisso Theatre was decided on: it was carried out in 1887 by the architect Montiroli who conferred on it the simple but elegant forms we can admire today.

## Spoleto and the Festival of Two Worlds

The Festival of Two Worlds (**Festival dei Due Mondi**), founded by Giancarlo Menotti in 1958 and based at Spoleto from the end of June to the beginning of July, is undoubtedly one of the most important and most eagerly followed international events of a cultural character in the world.

It comprises a series of performances ranging from ballet to opera, from theatre to concerts – especially famous is the "concert in piazza" held each year on the festival's final day in the magnificent stageset of the piazza facing the Cathedral –, all of them of the highest standard and performed, conducted and interpreted by major international talents, including those who have long achieved recognised standing in their respective fields, and those of the avant garde who have made an innovative but artistically valid contribution to the performing arts in our Time.

This is further confirmation of the extraordinary importance that has come to be assumed by this Festival and its high prestige at the international level. So great is its renown that opera and theatre buffs and lovers of art flock to Spoleto each year not only from every country in Europe but from the other continents of the world.

The Festival of Two Worlds is also combined with a series of other artistic events, in particular exhibitions of painting and sculpture and one-man shows devoted to artists of major international prestige.

In this regard, we cannot fail to mention the Festival poster, whose design is entrusted each year to a painter of recognised fame. They have included great names like Mirò, Manzù, Shann, Capogrossi, Folon and Afro, just to mention a few.

*FOTO DE FURIA*

**THE CHURCH OF SAN PIETRO.** Situated just outside Spoleto, close to the massive ramparts of the Rocca, the church of San Pietro proudly and magnificently stands on top of a high flight of steps.

## The Rocca and the Ponte delle Torri

The construction of the Rocca dates to the 14th century, i.e. to the period when the Ecclesiastical State sent its legate Albornoz to the town in the bid to quell civil dissension within it. It was Albornoz who commissioned the building of the fortress and who turned it into the bastion of papal authority. It was built by the architect Gattapone and enlarged and embellished in subsequent centuries.

During the Renaissance, the Rocca was the seat of illustrious, and sometimes notorious, personages, such as the ill-famed Lucrezia Borgia and her brother Cesare (the illegitimate children of Pope Alexander VI). It became not only a citadel of papal power, but also a splendid court: in fact, under Pope Nicholas V in the 15th century, its interior was transformed – probably by the architect Rossellino – and made more luxurious and comfortable.

Another wonderful and imposing construction is the **Ponte delle Torri**, the medieval bridge which joins the hill of Sant'Elia, on which the Rocca stands, to Monteluco. It rests on ten massive arches which boldly span the deep ravine below – a spectacular and impressive piece of engineering. The building of the bridge is almost certainly attributable to a period preceding that of the Rocca. But it is likely that the same architect, Gattapone, was responsible for its design.

## Monteluco

The wooded mountain of Monteluco, rising behind Spoleto, is a must for those wishing to explore the town's environs, both because it offers beautiful scenic walks through the dense woods of ilex that clothe its slopes right up to its summit, and because it has for millennia constituted the sacred wood of the area. As far back as pagan times it was considered a place holy to the gods; later, with the spread of Christianity, it came to be inhabited by many hermits who always preferred to live in isolated spots in order to meditate and pray and to remain in closer contact with nature. St. Francis, too, visited Monteluco and founded a convent here, simple and holy, like all the places where he lived.

Several hermitages may be found along the paths that wind their way up the slopes of Monteluco, including those of Sant'Isacco, Sant'Antimo and Santa Maria delle Grazie. Many caves in the rocks also provided an ideal shelter for these ascetic men. It was perhaps the age-old sacredness of this mountain that has ensured that its wonderful ilex woods have been preserved intact and at the same time made it one of the finest and most fascinating natural landscapes in Central Italy. Where man shows respect for nature, nature reciprocates by repaying him with beauty, peace and utility and by perpetuating the wonderful natural equilibrium that is the real foundation of life.

From the summit of Monteluco, and especially from its Belvedere, extensive panoramic views can be enjoyed over the surrounding countryside.

*Church of San Pietro*
*Monteluco*

*Opposite page:*
*Rocca (fortress) and Ponte delle Torri*
*Monteluco - Church of St. Francis*

# The Source of the Clitumnus

« *Hail, verdant Umbria, and you of the pure spring deified Clitumnus!* »

It is in these words from a famous Ode that the Italian poet Giosuè Carducci hymns these places that so many writers of antiquity had already extolled and admired.

The source of the Clitumnus: an enchanting and inimitable spot, an oasis of exceptional beauty and peace. The natural springs, welling forth from the limestone-rock, and the landscape in which they are set, form an idyllic fusion of so many elements of nature. The lush vegetation, mainly consisting of poplars and weeping willows, is reflected in the crystal-clear waters of the little lake. Here the vivid colours create exceptional reflections: everything seems to hover on the border of fairy-tale and unreality.

Not unnaturally, the ancients – enchanted by this idyllic scene – supposed that the god Clitumnus, a river god who dispensed his oracles from the depths of the waters, resided here. It was here, too, that the Romans believed that sacrificial animals should be brought for purification, because they believed that only this lake, with the purity and limpidity of its waters, had the power to make them pure and spotless.

In reality, the source of the Clitumnus, magically transparent though it be, is nothing but overflow springs welling up from the depths of the rock below. Close by stands the **ROMAN TEMPLE OF CLITUMNUS**, a small but harmonious building later converted into an Early Christian church dedicated to San Salvatore.

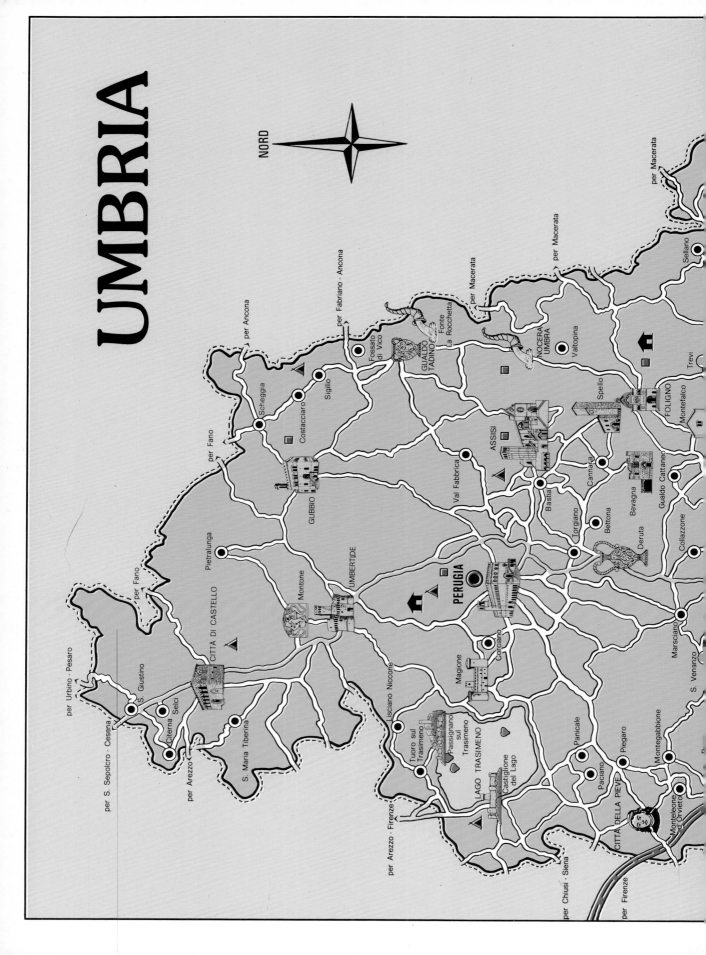

# UMBRIA

NORD

per Ancona

per Fabriano · Ancona

per Macerata

per Macerata

per Macerata

Fossato di Vico

Scheggia

Costacciaro

Sigillo

GUALDO TADINO

Fonte La Rocchetta

NOCERA UMBRA

Valtopina

Sellano

Trevi

Spello

FOLIGNO

Montefalco

ASSISI

Val Fabbrica

Bastia

Cannara

Bevagna

Gualdo Cattaneo

Collazzone

GUBBIO

Torgiano

Bettona

Deruta

per Fano

Pietralunga

UMBERTIDE

PERUGIA

CITTÀ DI CASTELLO

Montone

per Urbino · Pesaro

S. Giustino

Citerna

Selci

per S. Sepolcro · Cesena

per Fano

S. Maria Tiberina

Corciano

Marsciano

per Arezzo

Lisciano Niccone

Magione

S. Venanzo

Tuoro sul Trasimeno

Passignano sul Trasimeno

LAGO TRASIMENO

Castiglione del Lago

Panicale

Paciano

Piegaro

Montegabbione

CITTÀ DELLA PIEVE

Monteleone d'Orvieto

per Arezzo · Firenze

per Chiusi · Siena

per Firenze

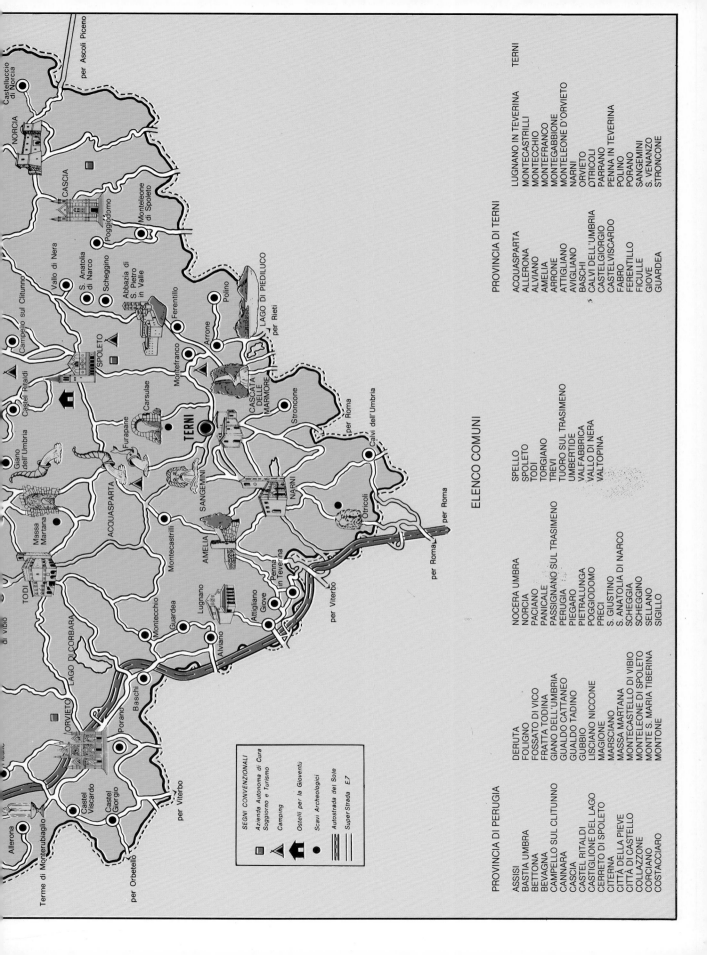

**SEGNI CONVENZIONALI**

- Azienda Autonoma di Cura Soggiorno e Turismo
- Camping
- Ostelli per la Gioventù
- Scavi Archeologici
- Autostrada del Sole
- Super-Strada E.7

## ELENCO COMUNI

### PROVINCIA DI PERUGIA

ASSISI
BASTIA UMBRA
BETTONA
BEVAGNA
CAMPELLO SUL CLITUNNO
CANNARA
CASCIA
CASTEL RITALDI
CASTIGLIONE DEL LAGO
CERRETO DI SPOLETO
CITERNA
CITTÀ DELLA PIEVE
CITTÀ DI CASTELLO
COLLAZZONE
CORCIANO
COSTACCIARO

DERUTA
FOLIGNO
FOSSATO DI VICO
FRATTA TODINA
GIANO DELL'UMBRIA
GUALDO CATTANEO
GUALDO TADINO
GUBBIO
LISCIANO NICCONE
MAGIONE
MARSCIANO
MASSA MARTANA
MONTECASTELLO DI VIBIO
MONTELEONE DI SPOLETO
MONTE S. MARIA TIBERINA
MONTONE

NOCERA UMBRA
NORCIA
PACIANO
PANICALE
PASSIGNANO SUL TRASIMENO
PERUGIA
PIEGARO
PIETRALUNGA
POGGIODOMO
PRECI
S. GIUSTINO
S. ANATOLIA DI NARCO
SCHEGGIA
SCHEGGINO
SELLANO
SIGILLO

SPELLO
SPOLETO
TODI
TORGIANO
TREVI
TUORO SUL TRASIMENO
UMBERTIDE
VALFABBRICA
VALLO DI NERA
VALTOPINA

### PROVINCIA DI TERNI

ACQUASPARTA
ALLERONA
ALVIANO
AMELIA
ARRONE
ATTIGLIANO
AVIGLIANO
BASCHI
CALVI DELL'UMBRIA
CASTELGIORGIO
CASTELVISCARDO
FABRO
FERENTILLO
FICULLE
GIOVE
GUARDEA

LUGNANO IN TEVERINA
MONTECASTRILLI
MONTECCHIO
MONTEFRANCO
MONTEGABBIONE
MONTELEONE D'ORVIETO
NARNI
ORVIETO
OTRICOLI
PARRANO
PENNA IN TEVERINA
POLINO
PORANO
SANGEMINI
S. VENANZO
STRONCONE

TERNI

# INDEX